24 HOVRS IN
ANCIENT ROME

24 HOVRS IN ANCIENT ROME

A Day in the Life of the People Who Lived There

PHILIP MATYSZAK

Michael O'Mara Books Limited

To the lady at the top of the tree – Barbara Hooley

First published in Great Britain in 2017 by
Michael O'Mara Books Limited
9 Lion Yard
Tremadoc Road
London SW4 7NQ

A CIP catalogue record for this book is available from the British Library.

Papers used by Michael O'Mara Books Limited are natural, recyclable products made from wood grown in sustainable forests. The manufacturing processes conform to the environmental regulations of the country of origin.

ISBN: 978-1-78243-856-4 in hardback print format
ISBN: 978-1-78243-857-1 in ebook format

1 3 5 7 9 10 8 6 4 2

Designed and typeset by Jade Wheaton

Printed and bound by CPI Group (UK) Ltd, Croydon, CR0 4YY

Follow us on Twitter @OMaraBooks

www.mombooks.com

CONTENTS

INTRODUCTION 7

HORA NOCTIS VI (00.00–01.00)
THE WATCHMAN HANDLES A COMPLAINT 11

HORA NOCTIS VII (01.00–02.00)
THE CARTER IN A JAM 20

HORA NOCTIS VIII (02.00–03.00)
THE BAKER STARTS WORK 29

HORA NOCTIS IX (03.00–04.00)
THE SLAVE GIRL PREPARES BREAKFAST 41

HORA NOCTIS X (04.00–05.00)
THE MOTHER CARES FOR HER SICK BABY 50

HORA NOCTIS XI (05.00–06.00)
THE IMPERIAL MESSENGER SETS OFF FOR BRITAIN 59

HORA NOCTIS XII (06.00–07.00)
THE SCHOOLBOY STARTS MORNING CLASS 70

HORA I (07.00–08.00)
THE SENATOR GOES TO MEET HIS PATRON 80

HORA II (08.00–09.00)
THE VESTAL VIRGIN GATHERS WATER 91

HORA III (09.00–10.00)
THE JURIST CONSULTS ON A CASE 102

HORA IV (10.00–11.00)
THE TEENAGER BREAKS UP WITH HER BOYFRIEND 113

HORA V (11.00–12.00)
THE STONEMASON WORKS ON AN IMPERIAL TOMB 122

HORA VI (12.00–13.00)
THE TAVERN KEEPER AT LUNCHTIME 132

HORA VII (13.00–14.00)
THE WATER-CLOCKMAKER STARTS A PROJECT 142

HORA VIII (14.00–15.00)
THE BATH ATTENDANT CHECKS IN CUSTOMERS 152

HORA IX (15.00–16.00)
THE HOSTESS ORGANIZES THE EVENING 162

HORA X (16.00–17.00)
THE WASHERWOMAN DOES A LATE SHIFT 172

HORA XI (17.00–18.00)
THE COOK GETS FRANTIC 182

HORA XII (18.00–19.00)
THE PRIESTESS PREPARES TO SACRIFICE 192

HORA NOCTIS I (19.00–20.00)
THE SPICE TRADER SETS OUT FOR DINNER 203

HORA NOCTIS II (20.00–21.00)
THE PROSTITUTE FINDS A CLIENT 213

HORA NOCTIS III (21.00–22.00)
THE ASTROLOGER CASTS A HOROSCOPE 224

HORA NOCTIS IV (22.00–23.00)
THE GLADIATOR STRUTS HIS STUFF 235

HORA NOCTIS V (23.00–00.00)
THE PARASITE RETURNS FROM DINNER 245

ENDNOTES 254

PICTURE CREDITS 257

INDEX 259

BIBLIOGRAPHY 271

INTRODUCTION

It is early September in the year AD 137. Rome's empire is almost at the height of its power. The imperial eagles have been carried into Mesopotamia and Dacia (and back out again, in the case of Mesopotamia). From the Thames to the Tigris, Rome is mighty, feared and respected.

Most of the people we encounter in this book don't really care about that. For them, life is not about celebrating the glory of empire but about making the rent, coping with difficult relatives and the daily challenges of home and work. Rome might be the greatest city on earth, but those living here still need to navigate the traffic, get on with the neighbours and find good, reasonably priced food in the markets.

This book takes us through one day in the life of Hadrian's Rome, with the city seen from the very different perspectives of twenty-four of its inhabitants. We begin at the sixth hour of the night – rather confusingly, the Romans started the twenty-four-hour day at midnight, but began counting the hours of the night from the previous sunset. This is just one example of the many ways in which the Romans saw the world differently from how we see it today.

From the viewpoint of the modern reader, many of the people described here live short, squalid lives in an unjust and highly unequal society. Death from infection and illness is omnipresent. Health care and policing are rudimentary, and most social services non-existent. Yet that is not how the people of Rome perceive things. For them, injustice and disease are universal hazards, to be endured and accepted. With all its flaws and inconveniences, Rome is still a better place to live than almost anywhere in the world. Rome has the same disadvantages as everywhere else, but its advantages are incomparable.

Not that the people of this city spend much time wandering about, gawping at their monuments and great civic buildings. They have lives to get on with, and it is into these lives that we take a brief look during this late summer day. Note, though, that our main purpose in doing so is not for what we can discover about the lives of individual people in Rome, but for what they can tell us about Rome itself. Because the Greeks and Romans believe that even should you take away the walls, buildings and roads, you still have a city.

The people are the city: the buildings and monuments later generations of tourists will admire are secondary, important only as the physical echo of the people who built and lived among them. For this reason there are few monuments in this book. The buildings we do encounter are not a set of sterile ruins but one part of a lively, multi-layered and challenging environment.

In the same way, the twenty-four men and women we meet today are not just the inhabitants of Rome – they, and hundreds of thousands like them, *are* Rome. This book is not an attempt to reconstruct the hours of the day for two dozen individual Romans – it strives to reconstruct a slice of the life of the city itself, reflected in twenty-four of its many thousands of facets.

While the people in this reconstruction are (largely) fictional, their lives are not. From the point of view of the modern ancient historian, antiquity is less about 'Great Men' than about the social infrastructure that underpinned those men and their deeds. Consequently, archaeologists, sociologists, epigraphists and those in a host of other disciplines have contributed to giving us an overall picture of how ordinary people lived and worked in ancient Rome. This book has drawn upon all these sources, and also upon the most valuable resource of all: the anecdotes, jokes, speeches and correspondence of the people who actually lived there.

The classicist will note where – in the cheerful knowledge that the copyright on these works expired centuries ago – the writing of a host of contemporary or near-contemporary Romans is woven into the text, from the letters of the erudite Pliny to lewd graffiti salvaged from brothel walls. As far as possible, the people of Rome speak of their experiences for themselves here and, for those Romans who had no voice in their society, this book attempts to speak for them. Often, examples of the original sources are given as excerpts, which accompany the main text, and in many cases the experiences of numerous individuals have been combined to depict one hour in the day of a single person.

The totality of these twenty-four hours is more than the sum of its parts. In the end, this book has only a single protagonist. That protagonist is the city of Rome – a teeming, bawdy, barely governable ant-heap of a place. Its flaws are many and sometimes horrifying, yet we nevertheless find in this city a huge energy and optimism.

There's an entrepreneurial spirit and an unflinching belief that, no matter how good or bad things may be, they can always be made better. In Rome, the slave strives to be free, the freedman to be prosperous, and the wealthy merchant to be accepted by higher society. While often complaining bitterly about their lot, the Romans are seldom resigned to it. They are dynamic, not depressed. They are convinced of their own superiority, and imbued with the feeling that, now they are here at the centre of the universe, they should make the most of it and kick and claw their way to a better life for themselves and their children.

Ancient Rome was more than a collection of buildings. It was even more than a society of interlocked communities of very different peoples and individuals.

Above all, ancient Rome was an attitude.

☙ HORA NOCTIS VI ☙
(00.00–01.00)

THE WATCHMAN
HANDLES A COMPLAINT

The fact that Petronius Brevis has a child – a daughter – gives rise to much ribald humour in the small apartment block that he calls home.

The wife of Petronius Brevis works at a fishmonger's stall in Rome's Forum Piscarium. As part of her job she has to supervise the transfer of live fish. These fish are brought to Rome at night in barrels of water. They are shipped live to avoid the problem of the fish spoiling during transport from where they were caught. Once extracted from the barrels, during market hours the fish swim around in shallow basins carved into the shop's stone counter-tops. That way Romans can get their fish really, really fresh. In fact, it is not unusual for a fish to be served at the table within an hour of its demise at the fishmonger's.

Getting the fish out of their barrels and into their counter-top basins needs to be done before the first shoppers hit the forum around sunrise, and this means that the wife of Brevis has to leave home an hour beforehand. Before she sets off for work she usually prepares breakfast and leaves this on the kitchen counter for her husband to eat when he gets in, although, given the hour he will arrive, he might view it as supper.

Brevis usually arrives home an hour after his wife has left for work, after which he eats his meal, has a quick wash and retires to bed. For Petronius Brevis is a member of the Vigiles, the Night Watch of Rome, and by that time he has been on his feet for the past nine hours. Thanks to their overlapping work hours, sometimes Petronius does not see his wife for a week. That's where the jokes about his daughter come from, as the neighbours speculate about how the conception was managed.

At the moment, Brevis has several long hours of his shift to go. He and his squad have a dual function: while the vigiles are charged with maintaining law and order on the streets after dark, this is really incidental to their main task, which is fire prevention. After all, the damage a violent drunk or even a murderous mugger can do is tiny compared to the havoc wrought by even a moderate blaze. Rome is divided into seven districts for fire prevention purposes, and Brevis and his colleagues are well aware that it was in the district covered by their cohort – Regio II – that the worst fire in Roman history began.

This was in AD 64, and the fire that started in these winding streets near the Circus Maximus eventually grew into a conflagration that was only brought under control six days later – by which time well over a quarter of Rome had been completely destroyed.

The Great Fire

On the hot, breezy summer night of 19 June ad 64, a fire broke out in one of the shops that lined the street-side walls of the Circus Maximus. As the historian Tacitus later explained, 'There were neither mansions screened by boundary walls, nor temples surrounded by stone enclosures, nor obstructions of any description to bar its progress.'

Tacitus – who experienced the fire for himself while a lad – gives this description from personal experience: 'The streets were clogged with fugitives. There were shrieking and terrified women, the disabled and the aged. There were men looking out for themselves or for others, some with the infirm on their backs, or waiting for them to catch up. While they looked back [the fire] attacked them from the flanks or from the front. Sometimes they escaped into a neighbouring district only to find it in an even worse state than the one they had just left.'

Many believed that so great a fire must have been helped along its way, and suspicion developed that the Emperor Nero had decided on the fire as a drastic form of urban clearance, after which he would rebuild Rome according to his own plans.

The jerry-built street traders' stalls, the warehouse sheds and the upper floors of many buildings are all of wood, tinder dry and jammed so close together that there is barely a single structure that is not touching another. All it takes is a coal spat out from a badly made fire, or an unattended oil lamp knocked over by a foraging rat, and within minutes a wall of flames might come sweeping down the street that Brevis and his squad are patrolling.

MODEL OF A ROMAN FIRE ENGINE. THE ROCKING LEVER OPERATED A FORCE PUMP.

Little wonder that the watch have the power to break into any premises where they suspect a fire might get out of control. As well as statutory powers to fine careless businesses or householders, the watch are not above handing out some basic physical chastisement as well. Given the huge danger that a fire presents to the neighbourhood, the epithet 'fire-starter' is among the worst insults one Roman can throw at another, and there is little sympathy for anyone at the receiving end of the vigiles' attentions.

Once a blaze has been detected, the unit has long-established protocols for attacking the fire. In the short term, they see to the evacuation of nearby buildings and organize a bucket-chain from nearby residences. All households have to keep a certain amount of water on hand for just this purpose, and Brevis and his men can tell you to the minute how long it takes for a bucket-chain to reach from any part of their patrol route to the nearest fountain. An unfortunate junior member of the squad is the designated 'blanket man', and carries vinegar-soaked blankets with which to smother any small fire before it gets going. If reinforcements are needed, the cohort fire engine will be pulled up. The fire engine is not a new invention – the ancestors of the machine used by the vigiles were putting out fires in Egypt centuries before. It was a Greek inventor working for the Great Library of Alexandria (a man named, appropriately, Hero) who first worked out the principles of a pump powerful enough to force water through a fire hose.

Every cohort of vigiles has specialists. There are, of course, doctors who tend to those roughed up by muggers and vigiles who sometimes come second in a bruising encounter with a large gang of thugs. There are also those injured by fires or by jumping from burning buildings (even though the vigiles also have a squad of 'mattressmen' who attempt to soften such falls).

If the fire engine fails, the watch will call in the heavy artillery, which is, well, heavy artillery. Over centuries of warfare and sieges, the Romans have become very good at knocking down city walls, and the ballistae, onagers and other artillery used for this purpose are even more devastating when used against standard (that is, ramshackle) Roman apartment blocks. So when there is a major fire, the Prefect in charge of the watch makes a quick decision on where the firebreak should go. Then the artillery let rip and create the firebreak with a high-speed demolition job. A four-storey building can become a pile of rubble remarkably quickly when subjected to expert targeting.

Once the building is down, it's the task of Brevis and his

colleagues to leap into the unstable pile of debris armed with long-handled hooks and drag out anything flammable. They have to do this at speed, since there is a fast-approaching fire at their backs. That this is dangerously exciting work is obvious, and this goes a long way to explaining the vehemence with which Brevis and his squad admonish those who carelessly set fires. (It also goes without saying that the former owners of the demolished apartments are seldom impressed with the Prefect's location of the firebreak.)

Fire Sale

Before the vigiles were organized by Emperor Augustus in the early first century, the only fire brigades in Rome were privately owned. One such was owned by the property magnate Licinius Crassus. In the event of a house fire, this public-spirited individual would turn up at the blazing property, firemen at the ready, and prepare to put the fire out – once the building had been sold to him. The longer the previous owner dithered or tried to bargain, the more the property burned its way to worthlessness.

'He would buy houses that were on fire, and houses which adjoined those that were on fire, and these their owners would sell for peanuts owing to their fear and uncertainty. In this way he [Crassus] came to own a large part of Rome.'

PLUTARCH *Life of Crassus* 2

Currently, however, the night is calm, without so much as a hint of smoke on the breeze. Brevis and his squad are leaving the via Patricus. This street is one of the busier thoroughfares of Rome by night, for it houses many of the capital's top brothels. Earlier in the evening the vigiles had to double back on their usual patrol route to move along a rowdy group of young aristocratic males who had been ejected from one of the brothels and taken their party out on to the street. On such occasions, Brevis rather regrets that his men are armed only with nightsticks rather than the swords with which the Urban Cohorts swiftly and lethally clear the streets during major civil disturbances.

Now it is just after midnight, and even the ladies of the night have decided to call it a day. At the side of the street only a few lamps burn behind the windows where the brothel workers have retired to their sleeping cubicles. It is the fact that the brothels have now ceased doing business for the evening that has brought the vigiles to the street for the third time that night.

A Roman magistrate, a gentleman of considerable importance and even greater self-importance, had attempted to stop by and visit his favourite establishment after an extended dinner with friends on the Aventine Hill. The magistrate was less than pleased to discover, firstly, that the brothel was closed, and secondly, that his regular girl had no intention of entertaining him so late at night. In a fit of drunken fury, the magistrate had attempted to hammer through the door with kicks and fists. This caused one of the girls to step out on to an upstairs balcony, pick up a flowerpot containing a small petunia, and shy it at the noise-maker's head.

Regrettably, she scored a hit, and the magistrate's howls of agony and outrage attracted the attention of the watch.

'I am the Curule Aedile, Hostilius Mancinus,' the injured man informs Brevis and his men. 'And I have been assaulted in the street.' The Aedile demands that the vigiles break into the building and arrest his attacker. Brevis sourly notes that the flowered garland from his party, which the magistrate is still wearing on his head, must have considerably softened the blow of the flowerpot, but nevertheless he is compelled to hammer on the door of the brothel until the frightened leno (Madame) lets him in. The culprit turns out to be a girl called Mamila, who sits sobbing on the bed of her chamber as Brevis takes her details. No doubt she will have to appear in court to explain herself, but Brevis is privately sure that, given the circumstances, no punishment will follow.

It is not as though the vigiles do not have a certain sympathy with the Aedile. Things falling, or hurled, from balconies are a constant hazard to those using the street below. The danger is particularly acute late at night, as those doing the hurling tend to assume the street below will be clear. It is not unusual for a member of the squad to return to his barracks in a particularly fragrant condition after some householder had been too lazy to wait until morning to empty his chamber pot in the latrines and instead simply deposited the contents out of the window without noticing the watchmen passing below.

Think of the other perils that wait at night.
The rooftops are a long way up,
and a falling roof-tile can brain you.
Think of the damage caused to the pavement
When cracked or leaky vases are tossed
Out of the window to smash into the road!

What kind of thoughtless, disaster-hunting fool are you

That you leave home for a dinner without making a will?
Every upstairs window along your route
Is a potential death trap.
Give a heartfelt prayers and hope that the worst that happens
Is that some local housewife dumps
A pail of slops on your head.

Juvenal SATIRE 3

←――――――――――――――――――――――――――――→

The watchmen proceed past the Circus Maximus and then turn south to patrol the small streets along the eastern slopes of the Aventine Hill. By day, there is reason to be wary here, for near the docks life gets rough to the point of being nasty and fleeting. However, the vigiles can relax a bit. Because most of the people on the east Aventine do not have much worth robbing, there are fewer thugs about, and dockers who have to be loading ships a few hours after midnight tend to be abed by sundown. The streets are narrow, dark and silent.

The silence of these streets makes it easy to navigate because, to the squad's right, just one road has all the bustle and racket of the morning rush hour. That's the stone-flagged road leading from the Ostia Gate to the Forum. Here an apparently never-ending column of carts clog the road solid, while oxen and carters bawl and bellow at one another and the squeal of ungreased axles adds to the cacophony.

At the moment, the chaos seems louder and more vociferous just at the point where the road narrows between the columns supporting the mighty arches of the Aqua Appia aqueduct that passes overhead. With quiet sighs of resignation, the vigiles turn downhill and go to investigate the latest problem complicating their night.

☷ HORA NOCTIS VII ☷
(01.00–02.00)

THE CARTER IN A JAM

Who but the wealthy get sleep in Rome? There lies the root of the disorder. The traffic jams of wagons in the narrow winding streets, the slanging matches between carters when traffic is held up – they make sleep impossible.

JUVENAL *Satire* 3.235

The Chthonic gods are the gods of the underworld: Mercury, Pluto and Hecate. On this night, as he does every ninth night of the year, Caius Vibius invokes these gods and begs them to inflict horrific tortures upon the souls of the authors of the *Lex Municipalis*.

The *Lex Municipalis* is the bane of Vibius' existence. The law is designed to prevent congestion in urban streets by forbidding wheeled vehicles within the city during the hours of daylight. As far as Vibius can see, the sole effect of this law is to prolong the congestion well into the night as he and apparently every other carter in Latium attempt to get into the city by moonlight and out again by sunrise. It's a stressful business.

For eight days out of every nine, Vibius is a peasant farmer who works his smallholding of seven acres, situated in the country south-east of Rome, not far from the tenth milestone of the Appian Way. It's a peaceful life, albeit one that features a lot of hoeing and a constant battle to keep slugs off his lettuces. Vibius goes to bed at sundown and wakes, rested and content, with the first birdsong before dawn. That's the usual routine. But then, every ninth day, Vibius is transformed into a morose, red-eyed monster who climbs aboard the family ox-cart and prepares for the journey into Rome.

The cause of this affliction is the *nundinae*. As the name implies, these street markets happen every ninth day in Rome. Though Roman housewives can get groceries at any time from the *macella* (indoor markets that are open every day) everyone knows that the produce at the *nundinae* is cheaper and fresher. That's because this produce was picked from the farm the day before and hauled into Rome overnight by long-suffering carters such as Vibius.

The actual selling of the goods is done by Vibius' sister-in-law, who lives in Rome. She has a spot on the via Mercatus, on the east side of the Aventine Hill, and a regular coterie of customers. These appreciate the quality of the produce on offer, for Vibius has a reputation for bringing in his best. Vibius' wife does her bit for quality control by ensuring only the best goods make it on to the cart. She makes sure that, for example, sub-standard radishes and other vegetables are fed to the pigs – who at around the time of the Saturnalia winter festival will, in their turn, make the trip to Rome as smoked hams and bacon.

The hard cash that the street market brings in is very welcome. Most of what is needed on Vibius' smallholding is obtained by barter with the neighbours, but particular farm tools, linen clothing and luxury goods require coin. Some of that coin comes from specialist traders. At different times of the year these traders make the rounds of the smallholdings in their carts, buying up the harvest and saving Vibius from having to make yet more trips into the capital. So the *lupinarii* have been around collecting the green beans and chickpeas, and the *peponarii* paid well for the family's melon crop. The *fructarii* make regular visits because cherries, peaches and apples ripen at different times. However, while the convenience is appreciated, selling to wholesalers at home is less profitable than dealing directly with the customers in Rome, so financial necessity dictates that Vibius still has to load his wagon every ninth day.

⟵─────────────────────────────────⟶

THE RURAL SMALLHOLDING

Juvenal to his friend Persicus:

And now hear my [planned] feast, and none of it is from the meat market. My Tibur farm will provide a plump kid, tenderest of the flock. One that has never yet eaten grass ... and has more milk in him than blood. Also wild asparagus, gathered by the bailiff's wife when she has finished weaving.

Eggs fit for a lord, kept wrapped snugly in wispy hay, served together with the hens that laid them. Also grapes which, though six months old, seem fresh from the vine. You will have pears ... and in the same baskets fresh-smelling apples as good as any from Picenum.

⟵─────────────────────────────────⟶

Today's cargo is fairly typical. There are lettuces in woven wicker baskets, a batch of early carrots (purple, of course, as the orange carrot is still a millennium away from arriving in Europe), unshelled peas, leeks and asparagus. There are six brace of hares, which were caught on the trapline that runs alongside the vegetable garden, and a basket of eggs saved up since the last *nundinum*. Vibius also carries goods to sell for the smallholders who live further away from Rome. These are less perishable items such as a variety of cheeses, pots of honey and swatches of coriander, parsley, rosemary and dill. It's easier for these more distant smallholders to bring their goods to Vibius by packmule than to cart them to Rome themselves. Their lower profit is more than outmatched by the convenience of being spared the final, most difficult leg of the journey to Rome itself – a sentiment Vibius appreciates all too well. It also helps that Vibius owns a pair of oxen – easily the prime asset of the smallholding, not excluding his house. As well as making the regular trip to Rome and ploughing his fields, the oxen pay their way through being rented out to other smallholders as the need arises.

It is quite likely that the oxen share Vibius' distaste for the trip into Rome. After all, they have to pull the cart. This cart is a triumph of utilitarian design, the type known as a *plaustrum* – the basic heavy goods vehicle of the Roman world. As Vibius can bitterly attest, no luxury has escaped omission in the vehicle's construction: it is basically a shallow box hewn from oak planks with an (un-upholstered) seat at the front. The wheels are crude disks of wood on to the rims of which strips of iron have been hammered in an only partly successful attempt to prevent the wheels from splitting every time they hit a pothole. While more expensive vehicles have some degree of suspension, this and most farm wagons have nothing of the sort. For shock absorption, Vibius has to rely on clenching his buttocks.

The axle barely deserves the name, being a pole held in place by two simple wooden bearings. However, both the axle bushing and the interior hub are lined with iron, which prevents wear. There are a set of iron washers around the wheel to ease friction, but the lack of ball-bearings means that Vibius' journey into Rome is regularly interrupted by the need to hop off the cart and slap another handful of grease on to the axle from a pot mounted on the tailgate for just this purpose. Grease can be made from pig fat or olive oil reduced by boiling. Either way, axle grease costs money, and Vibius only parts with a handful when he sees the oxen straining unduly. Until then the complaints of other road users about the squeal of metal on metal are treated with indifferent disdain.

The oxen were stoical enough during the late afternoon part of the journey, but as Vibius had resignedly expected they became more restive after dark as the cart approached the city. Like most Roman wheeled vehicles, Vibius' cart is intended to be driven on the soft shoulder of the road, leaving the hard, paved surface for pedestrians. But as the cart nears the city gates, the tombs crowd ever closer to the roadside (it is forbidden to bury corpses within the city, so the roads immediately outside are densely packed). The oxen are unshod and complain loudly when forced on to the hard paving slabs. Their indignant bawls when each unprotected hoof presses on a pebble add to the general cacophony of travel.

Long experience has allowed Vibius to time his arrival for well after the sundown queue to enter the city. He was actually congratulating himself on a slow but relatively smooth journey until his luck changed at midnight. Now, with a sinking stomach, Vibius eyes the stationary snarl of carts blocking the approaches to the arches of the Aqua Appia. From the general hubbub of shouts, curses and unhelpful suggestions coming from ahead, it is plain that a cart has shed a wheel and traffic will be at a standstill until the problem is resolved.

Cursing, Vibius readies the whip attached to a long ash pole, which, for most of the journey, has been used mainly to flick flies away from the oxen's ears. The plank sides of the cart have been raised by wickerwork to make them higher with just this situation in mind. Twisted backwards in his seat, Vibius squints in the faint starlight, ready when the first, small, grimy hand clamps itself to the top of the basketwork. The whip comes down hard across the urchin's knuckles and the would-be thief yelps with pain, which is followed by a very unchildlike stream of obscenities.

This is one reason why Vibius has taken a cart into Rome. The primitive axles and crude harness mean that the oxen cannot pull that much of a load without strangling themselves (the horse collar is another invention that is centuries away). In fact, Vibius could have loaded the same cargo on to five pack mules and done the trip to Rome more conveniently that way. However, apart from the rudimentary services of the vigiles, Rome is largely unpoliced, and one man alone with five mules loaded with easily traded goods has about the same chance of making it across the Aventine at night as a virgin carrying a purse of gold. Say what you like about the *plaustrum*, it does at least have the advantage of being a mini castle on wheels. Furthermore, the already ill-tempered Vibius is free with his whip in defending the ramparts, and after a while the urchins scamper off in search of easier prey.

There remains the more serious threat of gangs of older thugs taking advantage of the confusion to force the cart down an alleyway, there to be robbed at leisure. In such cases it is in the common interest of all carters to come to the defence of anyone so attacked. Vibius offers another prayer to the gods that this will not happen tonight, for while morally obliged to join in fighting off such street piracy, he knows the urchins will pilfer him blind while he is at it.

There is general relief when a team of vigiles comes down from the Aventine to investigate the fuss around the base of the aqueduct. Within minutes of their arrival, the stream of carts is trundling forward once more. As his cart passes under the massive stone arch, Vibius notes that – as is so often the case – the vigiles have been effective but unsympathetic. The cart with the broken wheel has been tipped on to its side in an alleyway where the now forlorn driver sits with his goods around him, hoping that his desperate summons for a carpenter will be speedily answered.

The sight reminds Vibius that at the next stop he should check the metal shearing pins that hold his own wheels in place. The torque between wheels and axle can cause these to break, bend or work loose, and this, along with the more catastrophic breakage of wheel or axle, is the most common reason for a breakdown. Thanks to this and the earlier hold-up, Vibius is already running late. A further delay would be disastrous.

Still, the venue for the *nundinum* is located not much further down the road, where a small stream of carts turns off, heading for the same street market at which Vibius will stop. It is not coincidental that so many carts are headed for the same market, as every trader picks a market as close to his side of Rome as possible. Thus market gardeners to the east of Rome will look for customers on the Esquiline Hill, and those further north will cater to the Viminal Hill. No one wants to travel further through the narrow streets of Rome than necessary, though some might make the extra effort to get to the Forum Holitorium, Rome's premier vegetable market, at the foot of the Palatine Hill.

MOSAIC SHOWING THE LOADING OF A LIGHT TWO-WHEELED CART

ADVICE FOR MARKET GARDENERS
Plant beans in strong soil which is protected from storms; vetch and fenugreek in places as clear of weeds as possible ... Lentils can

*be planted in otherwise unfertile soil. Look for red-coloured earth
and keep it free from weeds. Barley grows in new soil, or fields
which have fallowed. Plant turnips, kohlrabi seed, and radishes
in well-manured or naturally fertile plots.*

CATO *De Agricultura* 35

←───→

The location of Vibius' *nundinum* on the Aventine means
that since he has had to bring his cart to Rome, he will be able to
do a bit of extra business while he is at it. Some carters, with an
eye more to profit than hygiene, contract to load their carts with
rubbish, which they haul from the city on their return journey. This
has the advantage of allowing the carters to tarry in Rome longer,
because rubbish carts are exempted from the stricter provisions
of the *Lex Municipalis*. However, Vibius' second cargo will be far
more sanitary.

At the bottom of the Aventine Hill flows the River Tiber.
The space between river and hillside is taken up by the vast *emporium*
– the sprawl of warehouses and wholesale businesses that absorb
the flow of goods arriving from the Roman empire unloaded from
barges that have come upriver from Rome's seaport at Ostia.

The spring has ended the season of the *mare clausum* (the
'closed sea', during which ships from other nations are prohibited
from navigating here), and among merchant ships from Spain,
Carthage and Byzantium the first of the huge grain supertankers
from Alexandria have docked. These carry the precious cargo of
Egyptian wheat, which keeps Rome from starving. This grain has to
be distributed around the city, and it presents another chance for a
man with a cart to make a few extra *denarii*.

⚏ HORA NOCTIS VIII ⚏
(02.00–03.00)

THE BAKER STARTS WORK

After swapping cargoes and ascending some two-thirds of the way up the Aventine, the carter swings his team into a side road. This is far from the usual noisome Roman alleyway, for it is the service road leading to the rear of the premises of Misthrathius the baker. Unlike the average Roman side street, this one is paved with flat slabs of travertine stone and, furthermore, is wide enough to accommodate the cart without difficulty. The alley is actually lit – a pair of torches are mounted on each side of the bakery's wide gates. In front of the gates to the yard stands an impatient slave, who shivers slightly in a tunic too thin for the chilly night air.

'You're late,' he accuses the carter as he pulls up. The carter responds with an obscenity-laden description of his nocturnal travails. Nevertheless, by way of apology, the carter helps the slave unload the sacks of grain from his cart. There is a very strict hierarchy for grain sacks – you can't just stack any sack anywhere. The sacks from his cart get pride of place in the baker's yard, for they contain grain from Alexandria, imported all the way from Egypt.

Everyone knows that Egyptian grain makes the purest, whitest and – most importantly, from the baker's point of view – the most expensive loaves. Therefore, these sacks are carefully hoisted on to racks that will keep them clear of both damp and rodents. At the other end of the scale are the second-hand sacks carelessly stacked against the back wall under a rudimentary shelter. The cheap, Sicilian grain in these sacks is heavily adulterated with bran and barley and will be used to make *panis sordidus*, the cheapest, coarsest bread the bakery has to offer.

Like most bakers on the Aventine, Misthrathius does very well out of the Roman corn dole. Half a century before, the poet Juvenal remarked that the Roman plebs are bribed into subjugation by *panem et circenses* – bread and circuses. However, this is not quite accurate. The Romans are actually 'bribed' with a ration of wheat, which is handed out in the top tier of the former emperor Trajan's newly constructed market. However, no one bakes bread at home these days, not least because anyone starting a fire in Rome's highly flammable apartment blocks is likely to get lynched by his indignant neighbours. Instead, the poor take their grain to bakers like Misthrathius, who convert it into bread for a small fee.

Since the grain ration translates into about two loaves a day per family, and the baker has over a hundred such customers, it is no surprise that his bakery is pretty much a round-the-clock operation. It is also no surprise that, thanks to his baking skills, Misthrathius, who arrived in Rome as a slave boy from Cappadocia (where all the best bakers come from), is now both free and a quietly wealthy man. Baking is a good trade. Not only is the Baker's Guild (membership compulsory) highly respected among Rome's merchant classes, the bakers are even represented by their own candidate in the Senate. That senator's main preoccupation – and that of Roman bakers as a whole – is to constantly petition the emperor for an increase in the price of bread. Bread is the staple food of the poor and they get riotous if it becomes unaffordable. Consequently, the authorities tend to place a higher value on peace and quiet than on the bakers' financial well-being, and the price of bread is strictly regulated.

Today, as he has done almost every day for the past twenty years, Misthrathius has risen at midnight, and now, freshly bathed and shaved, he sticks his head into the yard to hurl his contribution of abuse at the carter for his late arrival. While he is at it, Misthrathius absent-mindedly picks up a hazel switch and whacks the flanks of the blindfolded donkey that patiently plods its course around the grain mill, which dominates the middle of the yard.

The donkey does not alter its speed one iota. It has spent most of its miserable life bound to the spokes of the mill. Trial and error have taught it the optimum pace for grinding the most corn for the least effort, and no urging by the baker or his staff is going to change that.

The mill itself is a fat cone, which, instead of coming to a point flares out again almost to its original width. The cone is hollow, and contains another, slightly more slender cone within. Grain is poured into the flared top, and is pulverised on its way down as the outer cone is turned by the donkey. A mixture of flour and crushed husks accumulates in a deep groove at the bottom, the latter of which slaves regularly scoop away.

Pompeian bakery, in (almost) working order.

The donkey's story

The following morning I was harnessed to what seemed the largest wheel of the mill. My head was covered with a sack and I was at once given a shove along the curving track of its circular bed. In a circumscribed orbit, ever retracing my steps, I travelled on that fixed path . . .

Though, as a human being, I'd often seen mill-wheels turned in a similar way, I pretended to ignorance of the process, and as a novice stood rooted to the spot in a feigned stupor. I hoped, you see, I'd be judged useless and unfit for that sort of work, and demoted to some other easier task, or even put out to pasture.

But I exercised that wretched cunning of mine to no avail, for several lads armed with sticks had soon surrounded me, and while I stood there, suspecting nothing because my eyes were hooded, they suddenly shouted all together on a signal, and laid into me with a flurry of blows, so scaring me with their cries that I abandoned my scheme in a hurry, tugged furiously at the halter with all my strength and swiftly performed the circuits prescribed, raising a howl of laughter at my sudden change of heart.

APULEIUS *The Golden Ass* Book 9, 11–13

←——————————————————————————————→

In theory, anyone can make bread. It is, after all, basically flour and water. In practice, producing a good loaf is devilishly difficult, and even on the Aventine there is a huge range in the quality of the bakeries. This is why, before each loaf goes into the oven, Misthrathius stamps it with his personal seal – no one is going to pass off an inferior loaf under his name. One reason a homemade loaf cannot compete with the professional product is because it won't rise. No one yet knows why bread rises, because yeast won't be isolated as the cause for another 1800 years.

What Misthrathius does know is that he has to leave aside a large nugget of dough from each batch after it has been kneaded. This dough is the leaven (from 'leave'). Bread without this leaven – unleavened bread – bakes into a flat, heavy and unattractive slab. But crumbled into warm water with honey, the leaven will, within an hour, develop into a frothy scum that will form the basis of the next day's baking. It goes without saying that every baker is constantly tinkering and experimenting with his leaven, and occasionally refreshing it with the must skimmed from grape juice in the early stages of fermentation. As goes the leaven, so goes the loaf – and heaven help the servant caught attempting to smuggle any of the precious stuff away to a rival.

These days we prepare leaven from the same flour that we use in making the bread. This is done by kneading the flour but not adding salt. Thereafter, it is boiled until it is rather like a thick gruel. Put this aside and leave it until it turns sour.

In most cases, the boiling is not needed, for the baker makes use of a little of the dough which he has kept from the day before. Clearly, whatever causes the dough to rise is acidic in nature, and it is just as clear that people who eat of bread fermented in this way are stronger of body.

PLINY THE ELDER *Natural History* 18.26

While leaven is the very heart and soul of his business, Misthrathius does bake a weekly batch of unleavened bread. He cuts this into flat squares and sells it as dog biscuits.

Within the bakery building there is controlled chaos. The place is, well, baking hot, which explains the thin tunic of the slave who was waiting outside for the carter. Most of the light comes from the wood-fired ovens just above floor level, so the room is lit like a scene from the underworld at a festival pantomime. On each side of the door stands a large, reinforced table with a basalt top. Almost the entire area of the tabletop is taken up by a deep basin into which flour, leaven and water are poured. Then, with the quantity depending on the desired end product, careful measures of salt and olive oil are added. The more oil, the fluffier the bread, and salt, perhaps with a tang of rosemary added, makes bread that will pair nicely with the pungent sauces with which the Romans like to spice their meals.

What gives the finest types of bread their excellent quality is firstly the quality of the wheat, and secondly the fineness of the cloth through which it is sifted. Some like to knead milk or eggs into the dough, or even butter. Such are the pleasures of nations free to practise the arts of peace and cultivate the fine skill of baking.

PLINY THE ELDER *Natural History* 18.27

A poorer-quality loaf will have the fine flour (*farina siligineus*) mixed with the inferior grains of emmer and spelt. Unlike some of his rivals, Misthrathius is well aware of the importance of kneading the bread thoroughly, and then kneading it some more. It takes considerable muscle to work the paddles with which the dough is prepared in the basins, and the job is usually done by two men per basin working in tandem. Given that they help themselves generously to the abundance of food that goes with the job, these kneaders might be considered as merely stout until one sees them casually lift a hundredweight of dough out of the basin and set it on a marble slab, to be divided into head-sized lumps and left to rise.

It takes about an hour in the fuggy warmth of the bakery before the lumps of dough have swelled to twice their original size. Now the dough needs to be flattened and put into its final shape.

Of the kinds of bread that are made we find that they get their names in various ways.

Some come from the food they are usually eaten with – for example, Oyster Bread.

Others get their name from their refined ingredients – such as Cake Bread.

Then we get Speusticus, which can be made quickly and so is called Hurry Bread.

Other varieties get their name from the manner in which they were made – for example, Oven-baked Bread, Tin Bread [baked in a closed metal box], and Mould-baked Bread.

PLINY THE ELDER *Natural History* 18.27

Before he went to bed the previous afternoon, Misthrathius had to spend around an hour strategizing which types of bread he would need to make, from what flour and in what order. When the fires have been unbanked and the ovens brought up to baking temperature there is no time for indecision – everything has to work with military precision. Risen dough needs to be baked precisely when it is ready. Leave it for just a little too long before putting it into the oven and what comes out – if you are lucky – is a collection of large holes loosely held together by a dry, crumbly crust. In the worst case, the over-expanded loaf simply collapses into itself and, anyhow, the sour, powerfully yeasty taste makes the failed loaf almost inedible.

So now the baker is everywhere – chivvying the men at the kneading paddles, back-handing the slave-boy who is lackadaisically shaping the loaves, and bellowing out of the window for more flour to be brought in from the yard.

He personally takes charge of the speciality loaves that have been ordered for today. This U-shaped loaf flavoured with sesame seeds will be shaped into a harp with breadstick strings to be served at a dinner party. A wedding dinner requires a large batch of loaves realistically shaped as male genitalia, for among the Romans the phallus is considered a symbol of fecund prosperity.

Other loaves are circular, about a foot in diameter and four inches high. The dough on the top has been slashed so that cuts on the loaf resemble the spokes of a wheel. This bread will go to retailers at the markets, who sell it by the segment, breaking off each chunk as it is purchased. Misthrathius sells a lot of these loaves and does not have the time to fit and remove each from a mould. So, with speed acquired from long practice, he loops a length of thick twine around the 'waist' of each loaf to prevent it spreading out as it bakes.

The bread of Picenum grows big with its white nectar as a light sponge swells when it has taken in water.

MARTIAL *Epigrams* 13.48

Whatever the shape, the loaf is placed on a flat wooden paddle, which will be used to place it into the oven. This occupies the middle of the room and is a huge arch made from flat, clay bricks. The space beneath the arch is bricked into two separate ovens, back-to-back and each secured with solid iron doors. Judging that the present batch baking within is done, Misthrathius throws open the doors and sends a blast of heat into the room. The brown loaves are hastily shovelled out into wicker baskets, and the new loaves stacked within, starting at the bottom shelf – which is less hot and where the smaller loaves and buns are cooked – to the top, where the large loaves are baked.

Every half-hour each oven disgorges another dozen loaves, which the baker's daughter takes to the shopfront facing the main street and stacks carefully on the shelves by bread-type. Despite the early hour, there is already a small crowd waiting for the bakery's doors to open. There is a group of watchmen, who time their rounds so as to be passing just as the coarse but tasty millet loaves hit the shelves. The watchmen mingle with sweaty workmen, who are grabbing a loaf before heading home after the late shift unloading barges from the Aventine docks. Among the other regulars is a young slave girl. As every day, she's there to pick up the large white loaf that will be part of her master's breakfast.

The Herculaneum loaf

Early on the morning of 24 August in the year AD 79, a loaf was placed in the brick ovens of a bakery in the town of Herculaneum. The loaf was designated for Celer, the slave of Quintus Granius Verus. It never reached its destination, as Celer, the baker and most of the rest of the population of Herculaneum were killed by the pyroclastic flow from Mt Vesuvius that destroyed the town.

However, the design of a brick oven is as good at keeping heat out as it is at retaining it within, and the loaf itself survived – though baked to the point of carbonization. The loaf is of the round 'cake type' described previously, with the top slashed so that it can be broken into eight segments.

The loaf has been scientifically analysed, and the recipe recreated. This particular loaf is sourdough, and though Celer the slave would have been unaware of this, sourdough depends on two types of wild yeast, Lactobacillus and Acetobacillus.

These can be encouraged to ferment by simply leaving a mixture of flour and water on the kitchen table for a few days (topping up the ingredients as required). Then once you have your leaven, add:

Half a litre of water

400g (14 oz) of spelt flour
(if you can't find this, use pizza flour)

400g of wholemeal flour

A tablespoon of rye flour, if you have it

A tablespoon of olive oil

Once all these have been mixed, you will have a large lump of dough that is slightly sticky to the touch. Let it rest for 45 minutes in a warm, humid place, and then knead again, this time adding a teaspoonful of salt. Put it in your cake pan, press in your personal stamp, slash about 1cm-deep into the dough to mark the segments and allow the dough to rise.

After an hour, your bread should be ready to bake – do this for 25 minutes at 220 °C (428°F). Do not allow pyroclastic flows from nearby volcanoes to interrupt the baking process, and you should end up with a fine, crusty loaf.

THE SLAVE GIRL PREPARES BREAKFAST

As she leaves the warmth of the bakery, the slave girl looks upwards to study the night sky. There is a lot to be done before the rest of her household begins to stir. The first task, for which she has just purchased the bread, is a breakfast, which must be served hot. However, tending the stove must not get in the way of other preparations for the morning. Careful timing of these preparations will make all the difference between receiving a beating or getting half an hour of extra rest. Fortunately, it is a clear night, so checking the time presents no challenge. The slave girl's clock is brilliantly spread across the heavens.

In Rome, street lights simply do not exist, and few people burn oil lamps. Above the sleeping city the stars are visible in all their glory, and this slave girl is completely familiar with the constellations. She looks for the 'Dog's Tail', the star at the end of the constellation of Ursa Minor. In all the sky, this is the one star that never changes its position in the heavens. With the ease of long practice, the girl locates the star and notes the angle between it and the star cluster she knows as the 'Seven Oxen'. The angle between the Dog's Tail and the Oxen grows steadily more obtuse after midnight as the stars wheel across the sky. From her quick upwards glance the girl knows that the ninth hour of the night is well begun. It is time to hurry back down the street to her home.[1]

This is the only home the slave girl has ever known, for she is of the *vernae*, the class of slaves who were born in their master's home. Indeed, her looks and mannerisms strongly suggest that her father is the *paterfamilias* himself, the master of the household. The girl was probably conceived after his idle dalliance with one of the maids a decade and a half ago. Having a slave mother, and never having been formally acknowledged by her father, the girl was by law and custom a slave from the moment she was born, and has remained one ever since.

Her long residence in the home and her probable parentage give the girl some privileges, but her looks have also earned her the envy and spite of her mistress. The mistress has remained childless, despite her best efforts, and despite the fertility promised her by a variety of Greek *pharmaka* and Etruscan amulets. She sees the slave girl as a living reproach for her failure to deliver an heir for her husband. Today that mistress will be visiting family on the other side of Rome, and this brings out mixed feelings in the girl. On the one hand, she will not suffer from being given arbitrary tasks and punishments while her mistress is away but, on the other hand, she must endure the process of preparing her mistress's coiffure for her trip. This is one reason the slave girl wants to get home and speedily stir the house fire back to life.

THE CASE OF VERGINIA

In the early Roman Republic, a magistrate called Appius Claudius was seized with a passion for a young woman called Verginia. To take possession of the girl, he produced false witnesses, one of whom claimed that the girl was only adopted by her current father.

Verginia was, this man claimed, actually the daughter of one of the female slaves in his household. Therefore by Roman law, she was his slave. The man demanded custody of the girl, and Appius – who had appointed himself as the magistrate hearing the case – immediately awarded ownership.

Once Verginia had been declared a 'verna' – a house-born slave – she could then be sold to the lecherous Appius. The plan was thwarted by the girl's father, who stabbed his daughter to death once all legal recourse had been blocked. Here Appius had outdone himself, for, by his own decree, the father was not guilty of murder, but of killing a slave which counted as damage to property.

The outraged father went on to lead a popular movement which overthrew the government. Appius was arrested for his crimes and killed himself in prison.

Details in LIVY *Ab Urbe Condida* 3.44ff

On returning to the kitchen she will first strip off the long outdoor tunic that she wears belted over her shorter indoor garment. Hanging this tunic behind the door, she then revives the fire and retrieves the bread. This she places in a specially shaped clay vase, which will keep it warm and steaming for when her master arrives for a hasty breakfast. Once the master has eaten, the girl will stoke the flames higher to heat the curling irons for her mistress's hair.

Hair is very important to a Roman woman. The slave girl wears her hair in a 'natural' style, brushed back and held with a leather cord. This hairstyle immediately reveals her status at the bottom of the social ladder. A woman like her mistress, or indeed like anyone with pretensions to social standing, wears her hair elegantly styled, piled and coiffured in the latest fashion. It takes time and expense to achieve this effect, so the more elegant and elaborate the hairstyle, the more money and leisure is apparently possessed by the woman underneath it. The mistress is not alone in demanding that the slave girl should attempt to give her a hairstyle that can really only be achieved properly with twice the time and budget available. Consequently, the slave is miserably aware that she may well be slapped, stabbed with hairpins or even burned with her own curling iron if her efforts do not measure up to expectations.

To get the curling iron (*calamistrum*) hot enough, the slave girl will bury the hollow outer cylinder into the coals of the revived fire. Later, she will wrap her mistress's hair around the instrument's solid core and then place the hot outer cylinder over this. As with much else in the slave girl's life, careful timing is required. If the outer cylinder is too hot, it will damage her mistress's locks. Not hot enough, and the hair won't curl. In either case, the blame will fall on the hairdresser, and the girl will suffer. The slave girl's preferred technique is to let the cylinder get very hot and then cool it slowly back down to the optimal temperature – it is easier to delay until the cylinder is cool than to fuss with getting it hot again.

←――――――――――――――――――――――――――――――――――→

Hairstyles – *a Serious Business*
Her household regime is pretty much as cruel as a Sicilian tyrant's court. If she has an assignation, then she wants to be adorned even above her usual standard . . . That's bad luck for Psecas, the slave girl who – with her own scalp torn, and her breasts and shoulders bared – does her mistress's hair.

'Why is this curl out of place?' she demands, with the bull-hide strap right at hand to swiftly avenge the foul crime of a twisted ringlet. Sure, and you blame Psecas? Improbable as it seems, it's the slave girl's fault that your own nose displeases you.

At the same time, on Madame's left, a slave draws out the hair, and combs and coils it into a bun. She'll seek the advice of a slave of her [mistress's] mother's . . . promoted after long service at hairpins. First it's her opinion, then those who rank lower in age and skill will confer. You'd think it was a matter of losing her reputation, or even her life, so desperately does her team strive for perfection.

Finally, her head is weighed down with layers of hair, piled high over the forehead in tier after tier. It's Andromache [legendary wife of the warrior Hector] you'll see from the front; from behind, someone altogether shorter.

Juvenal *Satire 6*

←――――――――――――――――――――――――――――――――――→

While the fire gathers strength, the girl prepares breakfast. A Roman breakfast is a somewhat cursory affair and, indeed, many families skip it altogether. From long habit the girl knows what her master prefers. The loaf she has prepared is circular, already indented at the bakery so that it can easily be torn into eight triangular segments. The master will probably wander into the kitchen after his morning ablutions and tear off three of these segments, which he will eat with a handful of the olives that the slave girl is now carefully placing in a bowl on one of the kitchen side tables. Just before the master's arrival, the girl will have extracted the loaf from its container on top of the oven and drizzled it with olive oil to make it even more moist and soft. After a moment's thought, the girl also extracts some sun-dried goat's cheeses and adds them to the sideboard. The master may eat them or not, but if not, they can be replaced in the basket with no harm done for having been offered.

Now the girl turns to a large bowl of hulled oats, which have been soaking overnight. She drains the water and throws in three fist-sized lumps of crude white cheese. She adds an egg and, after a surreptitious glance about the kitchen, complements this with a half-ladle of forbidden honey. After vigorously mashing the whole lot into a sloppy paste, she pours it into another bowl and puts this also on the top of the oven. Later this will be breakfast for herself and the other household slaves, some of whom will be too busy during the day to have any lunch.

With all now prepared, the girl steps out of the kitchen to glance at the starry sky, which is clearly visible above the open atrium of the house. Lamplight is already flickering in some windows as the household begins to stir. Although there remains around a quarter of an hour before she can expect her master in the kitchen, from long experience the girl knows better than to appear idle.

She takes a leisurely stroll to her quarters and returns with a large hank of sheep's wool.

A Quick Roman Breakfast

120g (4.2 oz) of pine nuts

Honey

Ground white pepper

A small jar of anchovy paste

Two smallish eggs (if using quail eggs use four)

Start by soaking the pine nuts in water overnight. Drain the nuts and add to a blender with a teaspoonful of pepper and one full teaspoonful of honey. (To go old-school, use a pestle and mortar instead of a blender.) Heat the resultant sauce gently in a pan while stirring in around two tablespoons of anchovy paste. At the same time, soft-boil the eggs in another pan. (Remember that small eggs boil faster so 3½ minutes should be enough.)

Peel the eggs, and place whole in a deep plate. Optionally, the bottom of the plate can contain a thin slice of barley bread toasted until crisp. Pour the sauce over the top, and serve immediately.

Sitting on a stool in the kitchen, the girl uses a large metal comb to card the wool into evenly spaced silvery fibres ready for spinning. The wool has already been sorted, as the quality varies according to the animal, or even the part of the animal, from which the wool has been taken. This is coarse hair from a ram, and it will later be woven into a cloak. Because the natural lanolin oil in the wool helps to waterproof the cloak once it has been made, this wool has been left unwashed. To prevent a big greasy stain appearing on her tunic, the girl places a large leather pad on her knees and settles down to comb the wool until her master arrives.

THE MISTRESS MAKES A SELECTION FROM A JEWELLERY BOX HELD BY HER SLAVE GIRL.

Carding Wool

Start with a hank of wool shorn straight off your sheep. Wash it. Sheep tend to get more than somewhat grimy, and the dirt gets deep into the fibres. However, you want to keep the natural oils of the wool, so don't wash at more than 70°C (158°F). (Lanolin in sheep's wool not only helps to keep the final garment water-resistant, but the oil is also great for the skin.) Once you've washed it, let the wool dry completely in a warm place.

Next, take your carding paddles. These are like square ping-pong bats with one side covered with blunt pins. The greater the pin density the finer the wool will be, but the more effort you'll need to make when carding. So match the size of the boards to your upper body strength – this is hard work.

Cover one card with hanks of wool. Sit and place this card on your knee. Now gently work the other card through the fibres on the loaded card. Keep stroking in one direction, as the idea is to pull all the fibres into alignment. Repeat until most of the wool has been transferred to the stroking card. Then change the cards around and repeat. Eventually all the wool fibres will be lined up on the card.

Gently roll up the wool until you have a loose cylinder. This is called a 'rolag', and it is now ready to be spun into thread.

⚏ HORA NOCTIS X ⚏
(04.00–05.00)

THE MOTHER CARES
FOR HER SICK BABY

O gentle Ilithyia, who has the power to produce a timely birth, protect the matrons [in labour]; whether you choose the title of Lucina, or Genitalis.

O Goddess, multiply our offspring!

Roman prayer in HORACE *Epodes* 17

It will soon be dawn, and still little Lucius Curius has not slept. Weary and frustrated, Sosipatra, his mother, leans over the cot. Yet again, as she has done many times already in the last hour, she wipes a damp sponge over the child's reddened face. In response, the infant screws his face up yet further and adds another wail to the cries with which he has punctuated the night.

'Children are born, and then everything is full of anxiety',[2] as the saying goes. There is so much that can go wrong before the birth, during the birth and in the months afterwards that a normal birth and healthy infancy is the exception rather than the rule. Therefore, like every young Roman couple, Sosipatra and her husband, Termalis, wed with the expectation that they would bury several children in the first decade of their marriage. Ancient Rome is not kind to infants.

As do most working-class Roman girls, Sosipatra married in her late teens. In the ten years since, she has continually been either pregnant or nursing a baby. Yet for all their best efforts, the couple have just one healthy child. This is their daughter, Termalia, who is now seven years old. That's about two years after the age when Roman parents can be reasonably sure that their child will survive. That is, survive the illnesses that in Rome kill two to four of every ten newborns before they reach the age of five.

←——————————————————————————————→

CARE FOR PREGNANT WOMEN

This care has three stages. The first stage aims at the survival and preservation of the injected semen. The second is the management and alleviation of symptoms such as pica as these symptoms manifest. [Pica is the craving during pregnancy for non-nutritional foods, such as chalk or sand; the word comes from the Latin word for 'magpie', a bird that the Romans reckoned would eat anything.] In the last period, as we approach parturition, treatment aims at the perfection of the embryo and endurance of the birth.

Above all, one must be careful to prescribe foods which are easy on the stomach, things which are easy on the digestion yet do not rapidly decompose. Things like soft-boiled eggs, spelt [a kind of wheat] prepared with cold water or watered-down vinegar, or solid barley porridge ... Fowl are good, if not fat and with dry flesh (such as dove, thrush and blackbird ...) ... Vegetables include endives, parsnips, plantain and wild asparagus ... Apples and quinces should be baked. Raw, they are hard to digest, boiled they lose much of their value. Well crushed and baked, they keep their strength while becoming more digestible.

After the seventh month an expectant mother should cease the more energetic of her exercises, especially the jolting caused by being drawn in a cart. She should indulge in the other exercises with caution ... If certain signs indicate that childbirth is imminent, preparations must be made for a live birth, for the evidence shows that children born at seven months are capable of survival.

... The breasts may have become enlarged, in which case the nipples must not be rubbed or squeezed lest an abscess develop. For this reason it is customary for women to slacken their breast-bands to accommodate the enlargement.

Extracts from the second-century physician Soranus,
On Gynaecology 14.46, 51 and 55

Thereafter, of course, the usual hazards of city life can carry off anyone at any time. And while her parents count Termalia as healthy, currently little Curius is sick, Sosipatra has miscarried four times, and twice a child born with no apparent problems has died within a month.

In short, Sosipatra is a typical Roman mother. In the past, even Cornelia, the *materfamilias* of the most aristocratic of Roman families, found that the top-notch care given to her as a daughter of Scipio Africanus was not enough to prevent a total of nine out of her twelve babies from dying before childhood.

In Rome, a woman might expect to become pregnant over a dozen times in her life, and even that is not enough to keep the population stable. This is partly because many women – such as the only daughter of Julius Caesar – die in the course of their first childbirth. As a result, the population of Rome keeps dropping. Only immigration from outside prevents the city from eventually becoming a ghost town – with young mothers and infants making up the majority of the ghosts.

It's heartbreaking, the fate suffered by the two Helvidiae sisters. How sad that both should have died in childbirth, and in giving birth to daughters. I am really deeply grieved, and struggle to keep this controlled. Yet it is so lamentable that these two fine young ladies have passed away just as their lives were beginning, and in the very act of becoming mothers. I mourn for the infants left motherless, for their excellent husbands, and I mourn on my own account.

PLINY THE YOUNGER *Letters* 4.21 to Velius Cerealis

At least, as her husband constantly assures her, she herself is healthy. The foetuses that Sosipatra has miscarried all survived until late pregnancy, but the birth of their stillborn bodies did the mother no physical harm. These little corpses are now interred within the walls of the house, so that Juno Licinia, Goddess of Childbirth, knows that this is a household friendly to infants. Sosipatra can at least have more children. All too many of her friends have been rendered barren after a difficult birth – often, heartbreakingly, a birth where the infant did not survive.

The infant Curius was born in this very room. Where his wicker cot is now situated underneath the window was the hard-surfaced labour-bed, which anxious relatives brought up the stairs. Now, alone and nervously watching as her child struggles for breath, Sosipatra remembers the bustle and non-stop activity that surrounded the birth.

There were never less than four people in the room. Her sister was among them, of course, taking charge in her usual bossy fashion. She and the midwife had joined forces to prevent Sosipatra's mother-in-law from attempting to force a loathsome potion of powdered pig's dung down the expectant mother's throat (as recommended in Pliny's *Natural History* 28.77). The mother-in-law had, however, been allowed to place a mummified hyaena's foot beneath the bed, and Sosipatra was forced to wear an amulet warding off evil spirits. Also, despite her doubts about the efficacy of such items, she had duly clutched the stick with a vulture feather affixed to it, to which her mother-in-law attributed the successful births of her own children.

Naturally, Sosipatra's hair was carefully unbound, as was the hair of every woman who entered the room, but this was common sense, not superstition. Everyone knows that nothing must be knotted in the room where a woman is giving birth. The knot of a girdle or even crossed legs or interlocked fingers have an aura which, if sensed by the mother, will dangerously inhibit the passage of the child. Everyone knows that the child and the umbilical cord can get dangerously tangled. Therefore, because like calls to like, having knots or tangles in a birthing room is simply asking for trouble.

After previous tragedies, on this occasion the young parents paid for a professional midwife. Midwives more often attend the births of only the wealthy, because a midwife worth her salt costs at least as much as a good doctor. What this couple got for their money was a sensible woman who preferred the texts of Greek doctors to the anecdotal evidence and amulets of over-excited parents.

Post-natal scene taken from a Roman bas-relief.

It was this midwife who had ensured that when the labour began Sosipatra was escorted to the birthing chair. There, with a pillow against her back and her legs propped up on stools, little Curius had come into the world through the crescent-shaped opening at the bottom of the chair, with the midwife crouching to receive him. Meanwhile, at chest height, his mother grasped the chair's iron crossbar with a grip so tight as to almost bend the metal.

The placenta had stubbornly refused to follow until the midwife had guided it out. Like many midwives, this one had softened her hands with lanolin oil for just this sort of occasion, and her fingernails were clean and well-trimmed, so as not to infect or inflame the womb. After disposing of the afterbirth and putting the bloody birthing cloths aside for later washing, the midwife had to hurry away. Sister and mother-in-law were already arguing heatedly about giving Sosipatra a mixture of chopped earthworms in honey wine to stimulate lactation for the child's first meal. (Sosipatra recalled that the potion had tasted less bad than she had expected, and certainly little Curius had never wanted for milk.)

How different was all that fuss and argument and bustle back then to this lonely watch six months later. Sosipatra is alone in the room, as father and daughter have retired to the back room in an attempt to sleep. Certainly, a seriously ill child is not regarded as sufficient excuse for Termalis to miss work the next day. For all but the grieving parents, dead infants are an everyday affair. Even the great Cicero had remarked a century previously, 'It should be easy to get over a child who dies young, and if the child dies in the cradle, it's not even worth paying attention.'[3]

This slave girl, born of Fronto and Flacilla, was my delight whom I would hug and kiss. Don't let little Erotion fear the dark shadows and the yawing mouths of Cerberus. She was just that many days from finishing her sixth cold winter … May the soft turf cover her fragile bones, and lie lightly upon her, earth. She was never heavy on you.

MARTIAL *Epigram* 5.34

More recently, the philosopher Seneca had chided a friend who had taken hard the death of an infant son: 'Don't expect me to console you; I'm here with a reprimand. Instead of taking the passing of your son like a man, you have done the opposite. He was still a baby! You did not know what to expect yet from the child, so all you have lost is a little time.'[4]

Yet as Sosipatra knows, it is one thing to contemplate the death of a child in the abstract, but it is quite another when that baby has been the focus of her love and care for the past six months. Every day Sosipatra has held the child, suckled him and watched over him anxiously, and slowly as the months have gone by, she has dared to hope. Now those hopes are in peril as her child lies in his cot, his little lungs struggling for the air that he forces out in painful wails. Sighing, Sosipatra goes to the corner table and carefully pours a little more oil into the lamp that burns there, the small, flickering flame the only light in the room. Three times during the night she has refilled the lamp. This means that there will be no need for a further refill, since before the oil runs low once more, daylight will have filled the room.

With daylight will come Sosipatra's sister, and with her a breakfast of milk, olives and fresh bread. Afterwards, Sosipatra will be chivvied into the back room to collapse on the bed recently vacated by her husband, and the sister will attempt to coax the infant to eat a meal of corn pap mixed with milk and honey.

*To the Spirits of the Dead ... this sweetest, most delightful
and pleasing infant. He had not yet learned to talk. His
parents Termalis ... and Sosipatra made this [memorial] for
their most delightful boy Lucius Curius, who lived six months
and three days.*

ROMAN INSCRIPTION. (*Corpus Inscriptiones Latinarum* 6.17313 Rome)

▥ HORA NOCTIS XI ▥
(05.00–06.00)

THE IMPERIAL
MESSENGER SETS OFF
FOR BRITAIN

Titus Aulus Macrius is a man in a hurry. He is also feeling somewhat harassed, as his original plan would have seen him exit the city soon after midnight. However, express messengers for Britannia do not leave with the imperial post that often, and it seems that every clerk at the Tabularium on the Capitoline Hill had his own message to add to the imperial dispatches that Titus carries in a waterproofed satchel at the back of his saddle.

Now, thanks to bureaucratic delays and last-minute postal additions, dawn is already lighting the sky and the streets are starting to fill with pedestrians. Titus keeps his horse to a fast walk, but even then almost rides down a woman who is hurrying to the nearby apartments with a breakfast of olives and loaves. Another hour to get through the crowds in the streets, Titus reckons, then he'll be out over the Bridge of Agrippa and heading along the via Aurelia for the cool hills alongside the Tuscan coast.

As he spends less time in the city, Titus is much more aware of drawbacks that native Roman city dwellers take for granted. The smell, for instance. To put it bluntly, Rome stinks. Over there is exhibit A, that pile of reeking ox-dung recently deposited by a passing cart. This has, at least, the virtue of being fresh, unlike the contents of dozens of chamber pots dumped on the streets earlier in the night by Romans too lazy to trek down to the public latrines and upstairs again. This particular stink blends with the pungent general odour of hundreds of thousands of humans and animals confined very closely together, and merges with the smell of rotting garbage wafting from the alleyways. Every time Titus comes to Rome, he feels his sinuses cringe in horror.

Yet among all this are also the more appealing scents of firewood and fresh bread from the bakeries, and the more raspy aroma of charcoal from where the blacksmith's forges are being started for the day. Also – and much less pleasant – is the reek of the tanners' yards, carried into his face by the east wind from the Transtiberim quarter (that is, across the River Tiber). The acrid scent of the concentrated urine used to soften the skins is enough to bring tears to a country boy's eyes, and Titus, born in the Sabine hills, still counts himself as a country boy, despite his years in imperial service.

Titus is a *tabellarius*, which is the name by which imperial messengers are known (this is because most messages are written on wax tablet called Tábellari). More particularly, he is the type known as a *stratorus*, a class of messenger that derives its origins from the word 'saddle'. The *stratores* ride on horseback and are the fewest in number and the most expensive type of messenger. They are only employed by wealthy aristocrats, businessmen and – of course – the emperor. On most occasions where a dedicated messenger is used, he travels in a light carriage and takes his time – in Roman society the people one knows usually live nearby, so there is little need to send urgent messages long distances. Unless, of course, you are the emperor. Like the network of roads they travel along, the messengers are a part of the fabric holding Rome's far-flung empire together.

If all roads lead to Rome, then along those roads to Rome come messages from provincial governors with budget estimates, tax returns and troop numbers. There are reports from scouts of barbarian movements along the frontier, and messages forwarded from client kings just beyond the Roman frontiers. All these communications are absorbed into the maw of Roman administration on the Palatine Hill. Then, in response, messengers like Titus fan out across the empire, carrying instructions to administrators about whether or not to take military action, or to prosecute members of that annoying sect known as Christians, or whether financing is available for a governor's pet project, be it a bath complex or an aqueduct. Hadrian is a very hands-on ruler.

The Peutinger Map

In the year AD 1494, a scholar came across an extraordinary find in the city of Worms in Germany. This was a scroll, almost seven metres (twenty-two feet) in length. On this scroll were listed all the way stations (*mansiones*) of the Roman *cursus publicus* (the name given to the imperial courier and transportation service).

The scroll is not a map, as such, for the intent is not to show the land but the routes. So the chart is highly distorted in the same way that a modern metro map showing subway stations does not accurately reflect the geography of the city above.

Nevertheless, the table is an astonishing feat that depicts the location of over 500 cities on cursus routes, and over 3,500 way stations and other locations. As a result, it is possible to reconstruct almost day-by-day the most probable route that Titus Aulus Macrius would have taken on his trip to Britain. It is also possible to trace even more romantic routes, through the Middle East to India and Taprobane (as the Romans called Sri Lanka).

The ancestor of the map was probably a chart of the *cursus publicus* as drawn up by then emperor Augustus' henchman Agrippa. Over the centuries, this table was embellished and extended to become the copy we have today. This is now in the Austrian National Library in Vienna, and shows the *cursus publicus* as it was at around AD 430, or 300 years after the messenger Titus Aulus Macrius worked for that organization.

THE SLOW MAIL. A CURSUS PUBLICUS CART.

As his job description suggests, Titus spends a lot of his time in the saddle. He cannot carry a lot of mail (something which seems to have escaped the clerks at the Tabularium) but he can carry it very swiftly. A private messenger with a horse and cart might be able to carry hundreds of letters, but if the messenger is not sparing of his horse, he will only cover around thirty miles a day. On the opening stages of his journey, on the excellent roads of central Italy, Titus aims to travel twice that distance once he is clear of the busy streets of Rome. At top speed in open country, eighty miles a day is possible if the messenger exerts himself. All traffic on Roman roads gives way to a messenger if he carries laurels on his staff (which mean he bears news of a Roman victory) or feathers (which indicate that he must almost literally fly with the news; feathers seldom indicate glad tidings for Rome).

Travellers on the via Aurelia, like travellers on most Italian roads, are well catered for. In Hadrian's cosmopolitan empire, many Romans travel for business or pleasure, and accommodating these travellers is a small industry in its own right. Like other travellers, the private messenger on non-imperial business will look to eat and sleep at a *taberna*, a house whose function is often signalled by a board outside depicting an animal, such as a painted cock or elephant. On most major highways, these *tabernae* can be found every eight miles, and on less frequented roads, every twenty-four miles. Out in the wild lands before Mediolanum, near the Alps, you are lucky to find one every forty miles.

This is of little concern to Titus, for he will use the government facilities beside which the *tabernae* have established themselves. The reason he can travel at such speeds without killing his horse is because he swaps horses every eight miles at changing stations called *mutationes*. All the major arteries of the empire have these stations. After the army, they are one of the largest expenses of imperial government, for there are thousands of miles of imperial highway, each with its changing stations housing up to eight horses for use by fast messengers, reserves of mules and oxen for slower vehicles, farriers and grooms to look after the animals, and public servants to keep track of where everything is.

←――――――――――――――――――――――――――→

PLINY (GOVERNOR OF THE PROVINCE OF PONTUS
ET BITHYNIA) TO THE EMPEROR TRAJAN:
Until now, Sir, I have never allowed the use of the cursus publicus *for anything but administrative purposes. But now I find that it has become necessary for me to break this hitherto fixed rule.*

When my wife was told that her grandfather had died she wanted to get to her aunt as soon as possible. Under the circumstances I thought she might use the privilege [of travelling with the cursus publicus*], as I felt that you would agree that it was unkind to prevent her doing her filial duty.*

... Therefore, being confident of your good wishes, I have taken the liberty of doing what would have been too late had I waited for your consent.

TRAJAN TO PLINY:
You did me justice, my dearest Secundus, in being confident of my affection towards you. Certainly, if you had waited for my consent before using those diplomas which I have entrusted to you, then your wife could not have been sent on her journey in good time.

PLINY *Correspondence with Trajan* 10.120-1

Though vital for the functioning of the empire, *mutationes* are heartily disliked by the communities in which they are situated. It is these communities that have to bear the cost of running the changing stations located within their territory, and these costs are high. So high that the imperial government has on occasion tried to ease popular discontent with the *cursus publicus* by assuming the cost of administration. However, this is simply not possible for a perpetually cash-strapped administration for any real length of time, and invariably the burden is passed back to the communities in a game of bureaucratic pass the parcel.

The *cursus publicus* is not simply an imperial Pony Express, though this may be true of messengers such as Titus. He is part of the 'fast post' – indeed, as a *stratorus* he is the fastest of the fast. However, the *cursus publicus* also has a 'slow post', and this carries much more than messages. The slow post is usually responsible for moving family and household members of senior government officials to or from Rome, carrying soldiers crippled in battle home to their families, and providing transport to any other ranking official who is capable of pulling strings to get it.

For just as there is fierce competition among clerks to get their messages off with a *stratorus*, use of the slow post is an eagerly sought-after privilege. After all, given that travel is a tedious and expensive business, who would not prefer to travel first class at the public expense? As a result, anyone using a changing station is sharply asked for his diploma, the official document giving permission to use the post. The document is carefully checked, for forgeries abound. Titus, of course, has his own well-worn diploma. However, as a regular on the Rome–Londinium run, long-term workers at the changing stations recognize him by sight.

Mentally, as he urges his horse through the ever-thickening throng on the streets by the Circus Flaminius, Titus is already planning the later stages of the day's journey. Thanks to the slow start, he is counting on a late supper at Centumcellae, a pleasant little town on the coast not far from Tarquinium in Etruria. The thought of passing the night there causes Titus no great pain, for all that he is eager to make as good speed as possible. The *mansio* at Centumcellae is one of the more convivial way stations on his journey, and it is a pity that the delays in Rome mean that his arrival will be delayed until late at night.

Mansiones are larger versions of *mutationes* (changing stations). The rough rule of thumb is that there is one *mansio* after every eight *mutationes*. At a *mansio*, one does not only change horses; also on offer is a bed for the night, a decent meal and a hot bath to ease out the cramps and strains of a day in the saddle. There used to be a time when Titus' journey would have ended with the day's ride to Centumcellae, and the messages that Titus carried would be passed on to the next messenger in the chain. Certainly, that was the way that it was done in the old Persian system, which the emperor Augustus emulated when he first set up the imperial post.

In order to discover as early as possible what was happening in the provinces, he [the emperor Augustus] established way posts. At first, these were manned by young men at regular intervals along the main highways. Later, these were replaced by regular couriers with fast carriages. Augustus thought that individual messengers were most useful, because the carriers of dispatches had been on the spot where they were written, and so they could be asked for extra details as and when these were required.

SUETONIUS *Life of Augustus* 49

However, that was then, and this is now. In fact, the mission that Titus is currently engaged in is a very good demonstration of why the emperors prefer their messengers to carry their mail the entire length of the journey. Among the mail carried by Titus are messages to the legate of Legio XX Valeria Victrix, the commander of one of the legions currently building Hadrian's wall across the north of the province of Britannia.

It is not exactly that the emperor doubts the loyalty of this legate. However, Hadrian has many enemies in the senate, and he would like to be completely certain that the commander of an entire Roman legion is not among them. Therefore, as well as the official messages that Titus will carry to the governor in Britain, the messenger has been carefully briefed on certain delicate questions that he will put personally to the governor on the emperor's behalf.

On his return to Rome, Titus will, again, hand over the official mail. Then he will proceed to a little-known office on the Palatine Hill, where he will report verbally to the head of the government's *speculatores* the result of his private conversation with the provincial governor. This is why the emperors prefer to have a single trusted messenger go the distance. Under this system, not only is one man responsible for the security and integrity of the mail from end to end of the journey, but the messenger can also carry verbal communications too sensitive to be put to parchment.

As one such trusted imperial messenger, Titus has made the trip to Britain several times, and not always starting from Rome. Hadrian is a highly peripatetic ruler, and Titus still recalls with a shudder those long hauls from Egypt to Britain when the emperor was visiting the former province. Long-distance summer travel is quite literally a breeze, for the prevailing winds blow from east to west across the Mediterranean, and all a messenger need do is wave his diploma to get passage on the huge grain supertankers that ply the Alexandria–Ostia route.

In winter, however, it's a different story. During this time a messenger from Egypt needs to travel up the coast of the Levant, and swerve inland to get through the Persian Gates to the Anatolian interior and avoid the impassably rocky coast of Cilicia. Then, for a while, the imperial messenger rides the same Royal Road that his predecessors used over half a millennium before when they carried news of Persia's defeat at Marathon, or later bore news of the death of Alexander to a grieving Macedonia.

At each *mansio* Titus makes enquiries of conditions on the road ahead. Gaul has been comprehensively paved over the past century of Roman rule, but Titus still needs to avoid bandit activity, roadworks and flooding, among other hazards. Given that he is now leaving the gates of Rome, it is not an unreasonable expectation that if Mercury, god of poets and messengers, speeds his way, Titus will be eating his breakfast in the governor's mansion in Britannia in three weeks' time.

For now, Titus halts again. This time, of all things, there is a class of schoolboys with their teacher forming on the pavement and road in front of him. Consigning himself to patience, Titus waits as the flustered grammarian shoos his students off the road. Hopefully, the clerks at the Londinium end will be more organized, and Titus will be able to leave at a better hour when he starts the long return journey to the overcrowded city he is now leaving.

▥ HORA NOCTIS XII ▥
(06.00–07.00)

THE SCHOOLBOY STARTS
MORNING CLASS

Spiteful schoolteacher! Even before cockcrow you shatter the silence with your harsh voice.

MARTIAL *Epigrams* 9.68

As does every school day, Publius Phelyssam's morning starts with him anxiously watching the head count by his teacher. So far, there are fifteen in the class that has shuffled out of the way to let the imperial messenger pass. The *litteratus* – Publius' teacher – is paid by the pupil by the day. If he does not get twenty children in his class, he will not break even. This is a bad thing.

Firstly, this is because it means that classes will have to take place in the open, as now, rather than in the basilica opposite. The basilica is by far the better choice, as it is sheltered from the sun and wind and has benches down the side where Publius and his fellow students can sit. On days when the *litteratus* cannot afford to bribe entry for the class from the attendant who cares for the basilica, or when the basilica is in use for an official function, Publius and his classmates sit miserably, cross-legged on the pavement, with their wax tablets balanced awkwardly on their knees. Publius does not like it; it puts the rest of the class in a tetchy mood and the other users of the pavement are not very keen on the idea either.

The second reason that not getting into the basilica is a bad thing is that it puts the *litteratus* in a foul mood, and he takes this out on his students. If the teacher knew he had been nicknamed 'Orbilius' by the class, he might have actually been rather pleased. That was the name of the teacher of the poet Horace – whom he nicknamed 'the flogger' (*plagosus*), for the freedom with which he used his whip. Publius' teacher also certainly never holds back with his whip – a short leather contraption that is constantly at his side – and like most Romans he sees nothing wrong with beating an education into his charges. That is why he would have been satisfied to know that some knowledge of Horace has stuck with his pupils, however derogatory the sense in which they have applied that knowledge.

←——————————————————————————→

What's a teacher's labour worth? Whatever it comes to
(And it's less than the pittance earned by a teacher of rhetoric)
From that the unfeeling pedagogue wants his bite ...

At least make sure you get something,
For breathing in the stench of lamps and boys,

While your copy of Horace gets discoloured,
And soot clings to your blackened Virgil.

Though it's rare you get paid without calling in the law,
Parents are savagely strict with the schoolmaster,
Demanding he be rigorous in his use of grammar,
Conversant with the historians and knowing great authors,
Like you know your fingernails.

…

They'll demand he shapes those tender forms
under his thumb,
As though sculpting faces in the wax,
He has to act as a father to that crowd …
It's not easy to watch all those boys,
Their hands and eyes quivering with eagerness,
And suspect purpose.

'Well, that's your job,' the parents say …

JUVENAL Satire 7, L216FF

As Publius re-seats himself on the pavement he is pleased to see another gaggle of students arriving. The teacher sees them too, though he makes a sour face at the sight of the *pedagogus*. Most of the pupils in the group arriving are between the ages of six and ten years old. This is far too young for them to be wandering alone on the streets of Rome, with all its multiple hazards, so most parents have their children walked to school by a *pedagogus*, usually a slave employed for this purpose. Sometimes all the parents on a block join forces to hire the same *pedagogus*, as has happened in this case.

ROMAN STUDENTS IN FORMAL DRESS

The *pedagogus* also carries the money for the children's lessons for the day, and the teacher's sour face is because he knows the *pedagogus* will not part with that money without being given a cut. Then, while Orbilius and the *pedagogus* are settling up, they are joined by another group, bringing the class to twenty-seven. With relief, everyone rises and they troop off to the basilica.

While I was visiting, a young man came to pay his respects to me. When I asked him if he was studying, he said, 'Yes, in Mediolanum [Milan].'

'Why not here?' I asked.

The youth's father had accompanied him, and he answered, 'There are no teachers here.'

'Why not?' I asked. As it happened, there were a number of fathers present, so I told them, 'It's of pressing importance for fathers that their children should get an education in their home town.'

... 'If everyone put in a contribution you could hire a teacher [in this town] for a small cost to each individual ... I would even promise to pay for it all myself, except that I fear my generosity might be corrupted to serve private interests, as I have seen happen elsewhere.'

'There is only one way to prevent that problem, and that is by letting the parents be able to employ the teachers. If they have to find a part of the wages, they will be careful to employ

*the right men. You cannot buy your children a better present
than this.'*

PLINY THE YOUNGER *Letters* 6.13

⟵⎯⎯⎯⎯⎯⎯⎯⎯⎯⎯⎯⎯⎯⎯⎯⎯⎯⎯⎯⟶

'Hey, Ba'al!' Publius is joined by a skinny redheaded kid who grins as he greets him. The boy is Casce, and he owes his name and red hair to a Gallic father. He and Publius share a mutual status as outsiders. As Publius' family name of Phelyssam testifies, the clan is Semitic, from the city of Leptis Magna in North Africa. Hence Publius' nickname: Ba'al. It used to be the more insulting 'Hannibal', but the mixed nationalities in the class can't really pick on anyone for their background, and if they do, it is their schoolteacher about whose origins they snicker behind his back.

Like many a schoolteacher, Orbilius is a freed slave, and even on warm days he wears a scarf around his neck to hide the slave tattoo that his former master had ordered he have there. It is because so many teachers are ex-slaves that the profession is held in very low respect by Romans. In fact, Orbilius is the lowest of the low, as respect for Roman teachers rises along with the level at which they teach. The basic Roman schoolteacher – i.e. Orbilius – is only a *litteratus*. He is generally deemed to have succeeded if he finishes with a student who can read, write, do basic arithmetic and has some knowledge of the classics. A hard-working teacher at this level – and Orbilius *is* hard-working, for all that he knocks his pupils around – might expect to earn around 180 *denarii* a year. That's about half as much as a skilled workman will make in any other profession. Even teachers of rhetoric at the level above Orbilius earn little more. No wonder the poet Juvenal once remarked, 'Many teachers have occasion to regret the unproductiveness of the professorial chair.'[5]

The 'professorial chair' in this case is a high-backed, rather battered wooden affair that Orbilius drags out of an alcove in the basilica and carefully embellishes with a worn woollen cushion. Publius and Casce stop a friendly tussle and hastily sit themselves to attention as Orbilius whacks the arm of his chair with his whip as a signal that they are to begin.

'*Defessi Aeneadae, quae proxima litora...*' intones the schoolteacher slowly while the children scribble furiously on their wax tablets. Dictating the *Aeneid* of Virgil is one of Orbilius' favourite teaching methods, as it teaches the children classics and writing at the same time. The Romans are very keen on learning by rote, and generally all a star pupil needs for success is a good memory.

Lucius Voltacilius Plotius is said to have been a slave and even to have served as a doorkeeper, chained to serve in his place as was the ancient custom, until he was set free because of his talent and interest in letters and became a teacher.

SUETONIUS *On Rhetoricians* 3

As far as Publius personally is concerned, the pious Aeneas and his heroic Trojans could all go and drown themselves in the nearest cesspit. He sees little use for a knowledge of the classics in his future. If he is to inherit his father's leather-working business, certainly he needs to know how to read and write, for the family still have business contacts in Africa and regularly exchange, for example, cheap cowhide for finished boots. The ability to write a good letter is essential here, as poor grammar or spelling indicates that the writer is a country bumpkin who could be exploited by a sharp businessman.

However, the business of declaiming rhetoric, or building elaborate verbal metaphors based on a pun involving Hecuba's mother, are matters left to those who will go on to the next stage of Roman education, where knowledge of the classics is essentially a status symbol. Unlike these aspiring members to the upper class, Publius fully intends to leave school the moment he reaches manhood in five years' time. At the ripe age of fourteen, Publius will formally shed his purple-bordered child's toga (well, actually, the family can't afford a toga and will rent one for the ceremony that welcomes him to adulthood) and don the plain white (and also rented) toga of an adult.

'Dull and unteachable individuals certainly exist, but like other monstrosities and deformations of persons by nature, they are few … If a good promise for learning passes away in time, this is due not to a lack of natural affinity, but a lack of care in maintaining it.'

'No [teachers] are more pernicious than those who, having grasped little more than the very basics, wrap themselves in what they mistakenly believe to be a cloak of knowledge. They refuse to yield to better teachings and grow fierce and imperious in their authority (this kind of person is usually puffed-up with authority). They teach nothing but their own folly.'

'Some say that boys under the age of seven should not be put to their studies, because until then they can neither understand what is taught, nor sustain the labour or learning it … However,

those of this opinion probably want to spare the teachers more than their pupils.'

QUINTILLIAN *Education of an Orator* ch.1 excerpts

←───→

Contemplating the occasion of his becoming a man, Publius absently fingers the *bulla*, which has rested against his collarbone almost since he was born. Every child has one of these – a little leather bag filled with the amulets and good-luck charms that took him through early infancy to achieving legal status as a human on his first birthday. It will stay with him until he reaches fourteen, when Publius will return the bag to his parents, just as his older sister did on the eve of her marriage earlier that year. The end of childhood, and the end of schooling. Publius can't wait.

Of course, this will not be the end of education. Like a good Roman *paterfamilias*, Phelyssam senior takes his role as head of the household very seriously. Sending his only son to a *litteratus* is only part of the boy's education, and in some ways the lesser part. 'Rest assured that nothing costs a father less than getting his boy educated,' remarked the poet Juvenal, rather snarkily in *Satire* 7. Indeed, Orbilius only receives a pittance for the lessons he is giving, but Publius knows that the education he gets from his father is the more important.

How to tell if bull hide has its native thickness or has been cunningly stretched to make the skin larger, and therefore more expensive; which drovers to contact for stock about to be auctioned for meat; how to take the skin off a dead feral hound and turn it into what the unwitting customer believes to be a pair of the finest-quality kid-skin mittens. This and much, much more is the education that Publius craves, and he can only get it from working alongside his father, not by holding his hands out to get whipped for misspelling '*defessi*'!

Sighing, Publius prepares for a long morning. Like every Roman schoolchild, he is completely familiar with the complex Roman calendar. Technically, his education might proceed for twelve hours a day, every day. Fortunately, there are usually some ten to twelve public holidays every month when Orbilius is legally prevented from teaching, and occasionally even longer holidays are decreed. For example, there's usually at least a fortnight of celebration every time the wandering emperor Hadrian decides to return to Rome.

Today, Publius has a full day, with only a break for lunch. Tomorrow he will only study for a half-day because he is needed in the workshop, and the day after that is a holiday. Meanwhile: '*Saxa vocant Itali mediis quae in fluctibus aras...*'

Dear Mr Schoolteacher;
Have mercy on your simple students. Well, do so if you want many shaggy-headed lads attending your lectures, and have the group that crowd about your table love you. Then there will be found no greater circle of students gathered around a teacher of arithmetic or a shorthand instructor.

Put aside your Scythian whip with its dreaded thongs (rather like the one with which Apollo skinned Marsyas), and that impressive cane which is your rod of authority.

Let both sleep until early October. Now are the hot, bright days of flaming Leo, and the heat of July ripens the burgeoning harvest. It's the summer. If your boys stay healthy through it, they have done enough.

MARTIAL *Epigrams* 10.62

☰ HORA I ☰
(07.00–08.00)

THE SENATOR GOES TO
MEET HIS PATRON

'But among kings and lords of all the world
the true man mingles undaunted,
Nor is he overawed
By the gleam of gold nor by the splendour bright
Of a purple robe.'

LUCRETIUS *On the Nature of Things* 2.5

The chanting of schoolchildren from the basilica brings this verse
to the mind of the senator as he hustles to meet his patron. The fact
that Mamlius Aurelius Ofella is himself also a senator of Rome, and
therefore technically counts as one of the lords of the world in his
own right, affords Ofella the occasional twinge of wry amusement.

Right now, Ofella does not feel like the lord of anything.

The fact is that Ofella is owned body and soul by a more senior senator – Lucius Ceionius Commodus. It was Ceionius who sponsored Ofella to the senate when he was simply a relatively wealthy but ambitious nobody from Spain. It was Ceionius who paid for the otherwise ruinous cost of staging games in the amphitheatre when Ofella was Aedile and rising up the senatorial ladder. It was Ceionius who introduced Ofella to his somewhat impoverished but highly aristocratic wife, and Ceionius who discreetly funded a large part of her dowry.

It would be nice to think that Ceionius did all this merely because he was a wealthy and philanthropic individual who befriended Ofella out of the goodness of his heart, and has looked after his best interests ever since. But if this were the case, Ofella would not be hurrying through the morning crowds to present his salutations to the man he calls his master.

← ————————————————————————————————— →

Come forward and tell us! When was your sleep more tranquil, now or before you became Caesar's 'friend'?

At once the answer comes, 'Cease, by the gods I beg you, to mock at my fortune; you do not know what a miserable state is mine; no sleep comes near to me.'

Therefore, when you see a man cringing to another or flattering him against his true opinion, you may say with confidence that he too is not free, and not only if he does it for a paltry dinner, but even if he does it for a province or a consulship. But those who do it for small objects you may call slaves on a small scale, and the others, as they deserve, slaves on a large scale.

*Then whenever a man can be hindered or compelled by another
at will, assert with confidence that he is not free. Do not look
at his grandfathers and great-grandfathers and search whether
he was bought or sold, but if you hear him say 'Master' from
the heart and with feeling, then call him slave, though twelve
fasces go before him [i.e. he is a consul] and if you hear him say,
'Wretched am I, that I am so treated,' call him slave; in a word, if
you see him bewailing himself, complaining, miserable, call him
slave, though he wears the purple hem [of a senator].*

EPICTETUS *Discourses* Ch.1 passim (Thomas Wentworth Higginson trans.)

Ahead of Ofella move several bodyguards, who clear his way by
the simple expedient of shoving anyone who tarries into an alleyway
or into the road. No one seriously objects to this, because Romans
are a very hierarchically minded folk, and Ofella is evidently a very
high-ranking person. The purple stripe on his toga attests to this,
as does the retinue that trails behind him. No doubt, thinks Ofella,
many of those watching his progress envy him – rather as he
envies them.

Perhaps it would have been easier for Ofella to take a litter,
a comfy, cushion-lined box carried on the shoulders of six sturdy
slaves. However, Ofella knows the dawn crowd on the streets,
and knows that a litter is even slower than walking. Once, many
years ago, the wife of the admiral Claudius was stuck in her
litter on an equally crowded street. In her frustration she
loudly vented her disappointment that her husband – a highly
incompetent commander who had just lost a fleet and thousands of
men – had not yet killed off enough Romans to thin out the crowd.
The sentiment was not well received.

Anyway, Ofella has ambitions towards military command himself, and intends to fish for a posting to the eastern legions while he is still with his patron. It would not do, therefore, to arrive lounging in a litter like some decadent dilettante (though his patron is sometimes accused of being exactly that by his jealous rivals). No, Ofella will arrive at his patron's mansion having marched there as he intends to march at the head of Legio V Macedonica, or wherever fate and the whim of the emperor might land him.

ROMAN SENATORS ON PARADE, AS SHOWN ON A 3RD CENTURY SARCOPHAGUS

For it is not every magistracy that frees its occupants – as well as their posterity – from their relations to a patron, but only that to which the law assigns the curule chair [i.e. those above the rank of plebeian Aedile].

On returning to Rome, he built a house for himself near the Forum, either, as he himself said, because he was unwilling that those who paid their respects to him should have the trouble of coming a long distance, or because he thought that distance was the reason why he did not have larger crowds at his door.

Plutarch *Life of Marius* 5 & 32

The reason why this morning's march is particularly brisk is because Ofella has been up before dawn dealing with *his* clients, and one of these clients had an issue with a client of his own that needed resolving. The problem was that a couple had divorced and one Julius Hypsates, the now ex-husband, as required by law, had to return the dowry. However, part of the dowry was currently invested in a merchant venture, and if Julius pulled his cash out now he would make a substantial loss. (Which, he complains, is exactly what his vindictive former spouse intends.) Julius had explained his problem to his patron, and the patron had taken the problem and his proposed solution to Ofella.

That solution was that Ofella should buy out Julius from his business venture, and that money could be used to repay the dowry. Since, as a senator, Ofella is not supposed to engage in grubby matters of commerce, the investment is now nominally secured in the name of Ofella's client – the ex-husband's patron. As it stands,

Julius' profit will be split three ways between himself, Ofella and Julius' patron, but at least he will not make a loss.

The System of Patronage

It is for exactly this sort of transaction that the client–patron relationship exists in Rome. This is also why no Roman, be he a street beggar or senator, would dream of being without a patron. Roman law is slow and expensive, and most legal issues are normally capable of being resolved without involving lawyers, provided that the client–patron system works smoothly. Pass a problem up the patronage chain high enough and eventually it will reach someone with enough authority to resolve the matter, or two somebodies representing clients on opposing sides who can force a resolution.

It is also why, as soon as he reaches any position of authority, a potential patron immediately starts looking around for clients. Not only do many clients add to a person's reputation, but – as Ofella knows all too well – clients are often the instruments by which the patron gets things done.

In the case of the wretched Julius, things were complicated by the fact that the ex-husband had dithered for so long that most of the paperwork had to be done right there and then. Which is what happened, but now Ofella has to proceed at a brisk pace lest he insult his patron by being late.

Since Ceionius is a very senior senator and a member of Hadrian's advisory council, he will evidently not be dealing personally with minor matters such as divorces and investments. However, he still needs senators such as Ofella as much as they need him. In fact, one of the reasons that Ceionius is a very senior senator (and rumoured to be a potential successor to the emperor) is precisely because he has so many clients. Clients in the senate will back any legislation Ceionius proposes and block any by his opponents. They can be expected to cheer his speeches, contribute towards his expenses and work hard to bring non-aligned senators around to the Ceionius position when there is a close vote.

As a client, even though he stands far above anyone else in the street in terms of power and prestige, Ofella is not his own master. His fate is out of his hands, and totally bound to that of his patron. If his enemies succeed in undermining him, then Ceionius will almost certainly come to a sticky end. Hadrian has executed almost a dozen senators who have displeased him, and Ceionius might easily join the list. As one of Ceionius' clients, Ofella would then certainly pay, though not necessarily with his life. Instead, for example, he may finally get that military command he is angling for, although it would likely be the less sought-after role as commander of a small garrison fort somewhere on the damper end of Hadrian's new wall in Britain.

Or, if it is felt that it is too dangerous to entrust Ofella with command of potentially rebellious soldiery, those who have overthrown Ceionius might suggest that, as the air in Rome is so unhealthy, Ofella might prefer to move elsewhere. Toma, for instance. The shores of the Black Sea may not be a happy place for a disgraced senator to live, but he might have to, unless Rome is the place where he wishes to die. The senate is ruthless with those who have fallen from grace, and charges of treason are easy to prepare against someone who will not take the hint and leave town.

Because the consequences of failure are so severe, Ofella, like Ceionius' other clients, works for his patron with true dedication. His colours are nailed to the mast. Even if his patron is clearly on the losing side, Ofella cannot jump ship. As he is required to do, Ofella has publicly and on repeated occasions acknowledged the favours his patron has done for him. Until those favours have been repaid in full, there is no way that Ofella can leave his patron without incurring that most damning of charges – ingratitude.

Yet while they are to blame who do not even show so much gratitude as to acknowledge their debt, we ourselves are to blame no less. We find many men ungrateful, yet we make more men so, because at one time we harshly and reproachfully demand some return for our bounty, at another we are fickle and regret what we have given, at another we are peevish and apt to find fault with trifles. By acting thus we destroy all sense of gratitude, not only after we have given anything, but while we are in the act of giving it.

SENECA *De Beneficiis* 1.1

For someone of Ofella's status, becoming known as an ingrate is social suicide. No one would talk to him, deal with him or protect him. He would be the whipping boy and scapegoat in every senatorial intrigue. Naturally, his wife would promptly divorce him, taking with her the dowry he cannot repay – an echo of the morning's dealings there – so Ofella would be alone, bankrupted and friendless. At that point he might as well take ship for Toma anyway, except that he couldn't afford it.

Ahead lies the property that Ofella has been briskly striding towards. As he reaches the large nail-studded oak doors, a servant hurries out to pull them open. Ofella's retinue peel away, ready to discreetly make themselves available again when their master re-emerges from his audience with his patron. It is not good manners to bring all your retainers into your patron's property.

In the vestibule a slave helps Ofella to remove his street boots and cloak. While he is at it, Ofella makes discreet enquiries of the slave about whether he is on time, early or late, and who is in the queue ahead of him. There is at least one senior serving magistrate there already; Ofella knows that because he has seen the lictors, the magistrate's attendants, lounging by the doors with their *fasces* – the official symbols of the man's rank.

Naturally, Ceionius will not call a magistrate by the insulting name of *cliens*. Even Ofella will not be treated that rudely. Ceionius will call them both *amicus* (friend) and pretend to be delighted by this social call. Indeed, the relationship between Ceionius and whichever magistrate is currently with him might easily have begun as a true friendship. Then the magistrate needed a favour, which only someone with the emperor's ear could arrange, and Ceionius was the one to arrange it. Afterwards, there might have been a small political difficulty that needed to be dealt with, which Ceionius had 'helpfully' ironed out.

If the magistrate could return these benefits with favours of a like value, then their relationship would remain as a friendship. This is, in fact, the essence of all political 'friendships' in Rome. *Manus manum lavat*, as they say – one hand washes the other. But when a favour cannot be repaid – ah, there's the problem! When this occurs, the status of the person who has received the favour slips slowly from *amicus* to *cliens* – and everyone knows it. Not for nothing do the Romans have the wry joke: 'I hate you because you have done so much for me.'

Ofella knows how his interview will go. There will be refreshments, of the highest quality. Ceionius will enquire politely about the health of his wife and the progress of their young child. Then Ofella, under the guise of passing on senatorial gossip, will report on his activities and those of his senatorial colleagues. He will mention how well he is doing in his allocated tasks of suborning one army commander, and discreetly bribing another. He will continue his hitherto fruitless task of looking for blackmail material on one of Ceionius' rivals and accept the polite rebuke for his lack of success.

Then, equally politely and with no hint of coercion, Ceionius will lay out the tasks he has in mind for Ofella over the coming week. 'If you could do this for me, my dear fellow ...' 'Would it not be a pleasant surprise if Marcus could somehow be persuaded to ...' 'I've never liked that Quintus. Would it not be sad if someone purchased his business and threw him out on to the street?' And so on, with Ofella smiling, nodding and busily taking mental notes.

First of all be sure of this – that when bidden to dinner, you receive payment in full for all your past services. A meal is the return that your grand friendship yields you; the great man scores it against you, and though it come but seldom, he scores it against you all the same.

So if after a couple of months it is his pleasure to invite his forgotten client, lest the third place on the lowest couch should be unoccupied, and he says to you, 'Come and dine with me,' you are in the Seventh Heaven! What more can you desire?

Now at last has Trebius got the reward for which he must needs cut short his sleep, and hurry with shoestrings untied, fearing that the whole crowd of callers may already have gone their rounds, at an hour when the stars are fading.

JUVENAL *Satire* 5.2 (G.G. Ramsay trans.)

←——————————————————————————————→

Ofella thinks back to the people he has seen on the street that morning, all of them surprised and gratified to suddenly find themselves in the presence of a Roman senator – one of the greatest men in Rome, when Rome itself is the greatest power on earth. What would these people think if they knew that in reality he was but a walking puppet, an empty marionette?

⚏ HORA II ⚏
(08.00–09.00)

THE VESTAL VIRGIN
GATHERS WATER

The *pilentum* is a splendid four-wheeled carriage, but open at the sides so that anyone sprawled on its luxuriously soft cushions can see most of the street. As a result, Marcia has a clear view of the senator Ofella as he leaves the house of his patron.

'Odious little man,' she remarks to no one in particular. 'Go on, duck under my carriage, why don't you?' Actually, despite her surface spikiness, Marcia is an amiable soul, and she would be rather distressed if Ofella did take that particular short cut. As the occasional street ruffian in a hurry has discovered to his regret, attempting to get across the street by ducking under this particular high-axled carriage carries a death sentence. The carriage is not sacred, but the occupant is, and anything that might be conceived as disrespect for her is generally fatal.

For Marcia is a Vestal Virgin. Much of her life is taken up by obscure rituals, and in the event of errors of omission (in ritual) or commission (in conduct) – by herself or others – draconian punishments as well. In fact, Marcia is on a religious mission right now. It's one she rather enjoys and has swapped tasks with one of her sister Vestals to perform it.

At the back of the cart are two large silver urns. Marcia is on her way to fill up these urns with the water that will be used to clean and purify the altar of Vesta in the morning ritual. There are certainly many sources of water closer to hand, but the water of Vesta should come from a particular sacred spring that is reserved for the exclusive use of the goddess and her attendants. This is the Spring of Egeria near the Capentian Gate. This gate is on the south side of Rome – in fact, it is the gate by which the famous Appian Way enters the city.

Marcia has taken a deliberately roundabout route to get there because she rather relishes these trips into the busy bustle of the metropolis. Another reason for the unusual route is to give condemned prisoners she may cross paths with a second chance. Every now and then, the guards hauling a man off to his place of execution – for example, to the Tarpeian Rock near the Capitoline Hill – might bump into the attendants of a Vestal Virgin as she goes about her duty. Naturally, the guards will give way – consuls, tribunes and even the emperor must do that – and then, if she wishes, the Vestal can exercise her power to free the condemned man right there and then.

Since those carrying out the execution have a certain sense of duty, they make sure they don't take their intended victim along the route usually used by a Vestal on her way to get the shrine's sacred water. However, Marcia likes to give her goddess a sporting chance to exercise clemency, and, like the guards, she does not take the usual route either.

As a result, she has glimpsed Ofella, a senator who has a minor priesthood that was granted to him by his patron, Ceionius. In Rome, priesthoods are political appointments, something the Vestals do not mind at all. This is because Vestals are mostly surplus daughters from highly aristocratic families and, as a result, they have the same keen interest in politics as the rest of their clan. Vestals attend a number of the banquets given by the priestly colleges, and these are a great chance to catch up with political gossip.

CHOOSING A VESTAL

But as to the method and ritual for choosing a Vestal, there are, it is true, no ancient written records, except that the first to be appointed was chosen by Numa. There is, however, a Papian law, which provides that twenty maidens [between the ages of six and ten] be selected from the people at the discretion of the chief pontiff, that a choice by lot be made from that number in the assembly, and that the girl whose lot is drawn be 'taken' by the chief pontiff and become Vesta's.

But that allotment in accordance with the Papian law is usually unnecessary at present. For if any man of respectable birth goes to the chief pontiff and offers his daughter for the priesthood, provided consideration may be given to her candidacy without violating any religious requirement, the senate grants him exemption from the Papian law.

AULUS GELLUIS *Attic Nights* 1.12 (trans. Loeb, 1927 ed.)

At one of these banquets, the greasy Ofella had attempted to bribe, cajole and threaten Marcia into alleging that a certain junior tribune had made improper advances to her. Since this accusation, if levelled by a Vestal Virgin, would have led to an innocent man being flogged to death in the Forum, Marcia had refused indignantly. Then the senator had implied that he might make the accusation himself, and allege that the dalliance was consensual.

This is a terrifying threat that all Vestals live with. Their virginity is sacred to the Goddess, and if a Vestal is unchaste, Rome will pay through fire, famine, earthquake or the destruction of her armies. Because even a Vestal ex-Virgin is sacred, it is forbidden to execute her. Nor could she be buried within the city (because she had sullied her calling) or outside it, because she is still a Vestal. Therefore, she would be buried within the city walls. And because no one is allowed to kill a Vestal, she would be buried alive. Actually, she would be forced to climb down a ladder into a small room carved into the walls. There, with water, a lamp and a single meal, she would be entombed and left to starve to death.

So no, Marcia does not like Ofella. She often wonders whether, if Ofella had followed up on his threat, the Goddess would stand up for her as she did for the Virgin Tuccia several centuries ago. Falsely accused, Tuccia had proven her innocence by taking water to Vesta's shrine. However, she drew the water from the river Tiber rather than the sacred spring, and instead of urns, she used the sieve with which the Vestals refined the sacred flour used in sacrifices. (This flour is called *mola*, and is why victims given to a god are said to be immolated.)

VESTAL VIRGIN 1ST CENTURY BAS-RELIEF

DEATH OF AN UNCHASTE VESTAL

But she that has broken her vow of chastity is buried alive near the Colline gate. Here a little ridge of earth extends for some distance along the inside of the city-wall; the Latin word for it is 'agger' [ditch]. Under it a small chamber is constructed, with steps leading down from above. In this are placed a couch with its coverings, a lighted lamp, and very small portions of the necessaries of life, such as bread, a bowl of water, milk, and oil, as though they would thereby absolve themselves from the charge of destroying by hunger a life which had been consecrated to the highest services of religion.

Then the culprit herself is placed on a litter, over which coverings are thrown and fastened down with cords so that not even a cry can be heard from within, and carried through the forum. All the people there silently make way for the litter, and follow it without uttering a sound, in a terrible depression of soul. No other spectacle is more appalling, nor does any other day bring more gloom to the city than this.

PLUTARCH *Life of Numa* 10 (trans. Loeb 1914 ed.)

Thanks to the goddess Vesta (and perhaps also to water surface tension and fine holes in the sieve) Tuccia did not spill a drop, and so was vindicated. Nevertheless, lack of chastity is something Vestals are routinely accused of whenever something goes wrong for Rome. In all the thousand-year history of Rome, though slanders and rumours abounded, only ten Vestals were ever formally accused of unchastity. However, the count goes up to eleven if we remember that the institution of the Vestal Virgins is older than the city of Rome, and the mother of Romulus and Remus – the city's founders – was herself a Vestal Virgin who claimed to have been raped by the god of war Mars.

Another time when the Vestals are suspected of their wrongdoing causing things to go badly for Rome is when it is believed that one of the Vestals has let the sacred flame of Vesta go out. This indeed is an offence of which the Vestals are more often guilty.

The number of Vestal Virgins is fixed at six, and the fire at the altar is not a large one. It must be fed regularly at short intervals and only the Vestals are allowed to do the job. This, therefore, takes up a lot of a Vestal's time. The chore is easy enough during the day, when a six-hour shift can be spent reading from a scroll, chatting with colleagues who pop in, and every now and then adding a few more sticks to the fire.

However, it is different when the Vestal has drawn a shift in the dead of night, perhaps after an exciting day at the Colosseum, or maybe even after watching the gladiators at the winter Saturnalia Games (the Vestals have front-row seats reserved for them). Marcia is far from the only Vestal who has then sat, nodding off in the stuffy room, and then awoken in frantic horror to find the sacred fire down to the last glowing embers.

The Pontifex Maximus checks up on this. Well, these days the Pontifex Maximus is both Rome's chief priest and the emperor, so he does not check in person, but he sends his attendants. If the fire is discovered to be out, then the emperor has the job of giving the Vestal a flogging. Before that he has to personally restart the fire by rubbing together two pieces of wood taken from a *felix arbor* – a sacred tree. This is a time-consuming, frustrating and finicky job that doubtless gives extra strength to the imperial arm when the flogging part of the ritual of redemption comes around.

Therefore, Marcia has happily exchanged fire-tending for water-gathering duties. Urns of water do not go out, and if they spill, then another trip to the sacred spring will sort out the problem. Of course, it does also involve little ceremonies and prayers to the nymph Egeria (whose spring it is) and these have to be done without error each time. However, Marcia is a second-stage Vestal and these minor rituals are second nature to her now.

A Vestal's career lasts thirty years and has three stages. In stage one, which lasts for ten years, the Vestal is a student, and if this seems a long time to outsiders it certainly does not to the student, who has to learn arcane texts, odd rituals and a surprising amount of Roman law within this time. (Unlike most women, Vestals can testify in court and are often asked to keep contracts, wills and other vital documents in their care. Also, a deposition sworn before a Vestal is as valid as sworn testimony in court.)

The next ten years of a Vestal's career are spent practising what she has learned. The final ten years are spent teaching this painfully acquired knowledge to the next generation. After that, it's done. The Vestal has discharged her duties, and should she so wish, she can spend the next thirty years painting the town red as she works off various pent-up frustrations.

In reality, no Vestals actually do this. In fact, very few even marry. The average retired Vestal is in her early forties, wealthy, independent and of an aristocratic family. Why such a person – among the freest in Rome – would then want to subordinate herself to a husband is something Marcia can't understand. Most ex-Vestals are of the same opinion, so they generally remain single and continue to live at the Vestal's shrine. If they do take lovers, they do this very discreetly, and elsewhere.

Also – someone has been counting – the statistics do not look good for prospective husbands either. For some reason, the husbands of those Vestals who do marry seldom last more than a year or two. The devout believe that even Vesta, gentle goddess of the hearth, is jealous of sharing with mortals those who once belonged to her alone. Marcia, who is keenly aware of certain illicit stirrings within her own body, secretly suspects that with some of these prematurely deceased husbands exhaustion might also be a factor.

The carriage bumps towards the Capentian Gate (it may be luxurious, but like all Roman vehicles of whatever type, it is also so poorly sprung that those thick cushions are as much necessity as luxury). Marcia idly ponders on the odd combination of circumstances that has a professional virgin collecting water from the spring of a nymph goddess who is mainly worshipped in the context of conception and pregnancy. (Egeria is also pretty hot on urban legislation, prophecy and earth-mother rituals, so as a goddess she has a remarkably mixed portfolio.)

Egeria's connection with the Vestals allegedly goes back to the second king of Rome, King Numa Pompilius. He was a cerebral, relatively peaceful type who enjoyed relaxing in oak groves. At one such grove, watered by the spring that Marcia is visiting, he met the nymph Egeria and friendship soon blossomed into a deeper relationship. Since a king was symbolically linked to the growth and fertility of the state, it followed that this growth and fertility should also be shared with the state through its goddess of the home and hearth, Vesta. Again, according to legend, it was Numa who founded the Shrine of Vesta, moved the Vestals into it, and gave them custody of the spring where he had met Egeria.

KEEPERS OF THE FLAME

Numa, upon taking over the rule, did not disturb the individual hearths of the curiae *[public or religious councils], but erected one common to them all in the space between the Capitoline Hill and the Palatine (for these hills had already been united by a single wall into one city, and the Forum, in which the temple is built, lies between them), and he enacted, in accordance with the ancestral custom of the Latins, that the guarding of the holy things should be committed to virgins ...*

And they regard the fire as consecrated to Vesta because that goddess, being the earth and occupying the central place in the universe, kindles the celestial fires from herself. But there are some who say that besides the fire there are some holy things in the temple of the goddess that may not be revealed to the public, of which only the pontiffs and the virgins have knowledge.

DIONYSIUS OF HALICARNASSUS *Roman Antiquities* 2.66 (Loeb 1937 trans.)

It's hard work lugging Vesta's water-filled urns back to the carriage, but Marcia regards this as a small price to pay for a few minutes alone in the tranquility of the grove, where the clamorous city sounds are filtered by the whisper of the oak trees in the breeze and the gentle splashing of the stream against the rocks. Now, urns filled and stoppered, Marcia slings her cloak over her linen *stola* and prepares for the journey homewards.

The *stola* is a simple form of dress that was popular in early Rome. Social pressure insists that the Vestals behave with dignity and dress simply but elegantly. As she reaches up to pull herself into the carriage, the Vestal Marcia is unaware that in two thousand years' time a massive statue of a diademed woman with the same clothing and pose will stand before the harbour of New York City holding aloft the Torch of Liberty.

▯ HORA III ▯
(09:00 –10.00)

THE JURIST CONSULTS
ON A CASE

The third hour sees lawyers active.

(**MARTIAL** *Satires* 4.8.2)

Although only the equivalent of 9 a.m., it is now the middle of the working day in Rome. The Vestal Marcia's carriage makes slow progress as the streets become steadily more packed with humanity. Romans are not just early risers, they basically live outdoors. For even some well-off Romans 'home' is often little more than a small cubicle in which to sleep and store clothes.

Dining and socializing with friends is done at the many cheap eateries and taverns that can be found on the ground floor of apartment blocks or just down the street. Bathing is done at the public baths, and the lavatories are communal facilities, again usually around the base of most apartment blocks. Entertainment is provided by street theatre, and for the more discerning types, by the participants in criminal trials.

As one might expect of people whose lives are largely lived in public, the Romans are highly theatrical and love the dramatic. The publicity of a good court case lets the participants put their backs into a real-life performance. Trials are held in public, and since even a case of modest theft – such as a cloak – can result in draconian punishment, the histrionics by defendants, their counsel and even the judge, all provide an intriguing, authentic spectacle for onlookers.

A condemned thief might end up in the arena wearing the *toga molesta* – a tunic covered in inflammable material that is set alight for the delectation of the audience. Hence the grim Roman joke, 'A thief stole a tunic. To hide the pattern he smeared it with pitch.'

Unsurprisingly then, anyone accused of a crime looks for the best legal representation he can find. However, it is not quite that simple. For a start, those representing the accused in a Roman court case are not professional lawyers. Well, not officially anyway. They are supposedly amateurs, in that they are meant to be friends or colleagues of the accused, and they are certainly amateurs in the sense that they are not paid for their work. (Of course, in reality someone accused will have asked his patron to find him the best defender possible and a patron might himself take part in a trial, in which case the defendant is his client in every sense of the word.)

Secondly, the average Roman court case is meant to start at sunrise and end before dusk. This does not give prosecution or defence a lot of time, so quite often many of the facts of the case are agreed beforehand, and both parties concentrate on convincing the jury about only the disputed details.

There's a lot of interest in the case currently being heard in the basilica, since it involves a well-known scandal. A slave woman poisoned her master's lover – a crime that she admits, but claims that she did so under the orders of her master. According to the slave, she acted out of fear of the dreadful punishments she would suffer if she disobeyed. The master denies giving any such order. He claims that the slave was once his concubine, and when he abandoned her for a freeborn woman she poisoned the new lover out of jealousy. This defence was widely disbelieved so the master is now on trial for incitement to murder.

The master in question is a well-known merchant, and the case has attracted quite a crowd of spectators. This crowd has packed the basilica, where there was not a lot of room to start with, even once a class of schoolchildren had been unceremoniously ejected. Apart from the Praetor (the magistrate) and his attendants, the accused and his friends, the witnesses and the jury, there is also the confessed poisoner and her accompanying guards.

As a result, the audience has spilled out of the open-fronted basilica into the street, and there impeded both the carriage of Marcia the Vestal as she returns with her water, and Gaius the Jurist, who has been summoned by the Praetor. As a jurist, Gaius is a member of the imperial bureaucracy and therefore subject to the Praetor's orders. This often means that he is called out of his scroll-packed office at short notice and ordered to consult on a case such as this.

At least today is sunny. However, Gaius envies some of his predecessors in his role, men such as Mucius Scaevola, who were wealthy, aristocratic amateurs. Their interest in the law was purely academic. They did not get pulled out of their studies at short notice to get involved with actual trials involving real people. Though Gaius loves the law, he prefers to interact as little as possible with the humans to which it is applied. Certainly, he has no liking for shoving through a sharp-elbowed crowd, with people constantly jostling him and threatening to bump the scrolls out of his arms.

Gaius was rather looking forward to a quiet morning going through the legal letters of the emperors Augustus and Tiberius (*libelli*), and attempting to establish a set of legal principles drawn from the emperor's responses to requests for judgements on matters affecting everyone from private individuals to cities or even entire nations. Now, instead of spending a quiet morning with a dead emperor's correspondence, he will have to deliver an opinion on some ghastly, lurid scandal of a case while the great slack-jawed unwashed watch on and shout unsolicited and highly unprofessional advice.

THE BASILICA AT POMPEII. THE JUDGE SAT ON A RASIED
PLINTH ACCESSIBLE BY A SMALL WOODEN STAIR.

The Praetor has been attempting to look stone-faced and stoical while waiting for Gaius to arrive, but is actually sitting upon his curule chair with ever-increasing irritation. Once he sees the jurist struggling through the crowd, he signals to his lictors to clear a path for Gaius to the court. Gaius can understand some of the Praetor's irritation. The curule chair might be the symbol of the majesty of the senior magistrates of Rome, but it is not a comfortable chair to be sat in for any length of time. It is not designed to be. Rather, the narrow, backless chair with its hard seat is designed to encourage the occupant to complete the state's business as fast as possible.

The Praetor is, frankly, getting tired of listening to the hysterical wails of the daughters of the accused, brought into court for just this purpose. With their hair down and dishevelled, and their teenage faces streaked with tears, the girls cling to their father's toga and beg the jury not to condemn him and leave them orphaned to face a cruel, uncaring world.

In keeping with the occasion, the father's toga is black (the colour of mourning, and this toga is indeed usually rented out for funerals rather than to the defendants in a court case). The father is unshaven, showing the world that he is too distraught to be allowed near a razor, and tears stream down his face as he beseeches his friends, colleagues and even random passers-by to care for his precious children should the judgement go against him. This has been going on for an hour now, and though the spectators seem to love it, the court officials are starting to look a bit jaded.

This is not even the trial – it's the preliminary to a trial. The Praetor is there because he, in his dread person, literally is the law. His first task when appointed Urban Praetor was to announce which of the laws embodied in the precedents set by his predecessors he would follow. By his judgements today and for the rest of his year in office he will make new laws for the coming generations. Since the Urban Praetor is not himself a lawyer, he consults very closely with jurists like Gaius and his colleagues before doing anything irrevocable. Apart from anything else, the emperor Hadrian has a keen interest in matters legal, and the ambitious aristocrat now in the Praetor's chair does not want to be seen as an incompetent by his emperor.

The magistrates of the Roman people have the power of promulgating edicts, but the highest authority belongs to the edicts of the two Prætors, the urban and the foreign, whose jurisdiction is vested in the governors of the provinces; as well as to the edicts of the curule Ædiles, whose jurisdiction the Quæstors administer in the provinces of the Roman people, for Quæstors are not appointed in the provinces of the Emperor and, therefore, the latter edict is not published in these provinces.

The answers of jurists are the decisions and opinions of those who are authorized to define the law.

GAIUS 1.6–7

This is why he has sent for Gaius. The first thing he has to decide is whether the accused is guilty of poisoning by proxy, or whether, in performing a criminal deed, the slave acted beyond the bounds of agency. There are some things you cannot force even a slave to do. If this is determined to be one such case, the accused cannot be held responsible for his slave's actions, even if he ordered her to commit the crime.

Things were easier back in the days of the Roman Republic. Then, a slave was a slave – no more than a 'talking tool', to use the words of Cato the Elder. However, in the more civilized world of the Empire, the law recognizes that slavery is an unnatural condition, and those subject to it – by birth or misfortune – are, nevertheless, as human as anyone else. Therefore, all sorts of legal issues have developed around the rights of slaves and their relationship with their masters. For example, a master can be forced to sell a slave whom he is judged to have treated barbarically, and a master who abandons a sick slave so as to save the cost of medical treatment is judged to have performed manumission by neglect. If the slave recovers, he or she does so in freedom.

In this particular case, by the Praetor's reckoning, the slave knew that being ordered to poison someone was blatantly illegal. Therefore – since the law these days recognizes that slaves are thinking rational humans rather than tools – her proper response should have been to report her master to the authorities. This principle – that a slave can inform on a master who is committing a serious crime – goes back to the earliest Republic, when a slave called Vindictus reported his master for treason.

That slave was proven right and judged to have acted correctly (which is why in future millennia a man proven to have acted rightly is said to be 'vindicated'). This precedent, reckons the Praetor, means that if the slave present before him today went ahead with the killing, it was not because of threats, but because poisoning the merchant's lover was fully in line with her own inclinations. Therefore, it was a voluntary action. However, the accusers – the family of the deceased – are also present and grimly confronting him. The Praetor wants the opinion of Gaius before he rules that a prosecution for poisoning by proxy is inadmissible in law.

It is provided by the Lex Ælia Sentia that slaves who have been placed in chains by their masters, or have been branded, or have been subjected to torture for some offence and convicted, or have been delivered up to fight with others or with wild beasts, or to contend with gladiators, or have been thrown into prison and have afterwards been manumitted by the same, or by another master, shall become free, and belong to the same class as that of enemies who have surrendered at discretion.

INSTITUTES OF GAIUS 1.13

His caution is especially called for in this case because the man prosecuting the merchant is well known to have a pretty good grasp of the law himself. Though ostensibly acting as a friend of the family of the deceased, the *Praetor* suspects that the prosecutor had never met a single one of them before the poisoning took place. He is, however, a well-known rival of the merchant in the dock and he would like nothing better than to choke off a competitor.

That choking-off, by the way, would be literal. If the *Praetor* allows the case to go ahead and the merchant is found guilty, then the death sentence would be applied automatically. Because the merchant is a Roman citizen, he will be spared the flamboyant punishments meted out in the arena or a horrible death by crucifixion. Instead, the prisoner would be taken to the cells of the Tullianum, which is Rome's prison, and once there would be quickly and unceremoniously strangled by an executioner. Slaves will then put a hook through the corpse and drag it down to the Tiber, where it will be flung into the river like so much garbage. That grim prospect is certainly enough to make the merchant's daughters hysterical.

Gaius has arrived to a speculative hubbub among the spectators. He is already roughly aware of the facts of the case, and the Praetor swiftly fills him in on the legal position taken by the prosecution and defence. The jurist nods his agreement with the Praetor's opinion that slaves cannot be ordered to commit crimes by their masters. Otherwise, Rome would swiftly descend into anarchy as masters ordered their slaves to rob, beat and murder others at will, safe in the knowledge that they could disavow their slaves if caught.

But perhaps, enquires the Praetor, the opposite applies. The master is in effect *in loco parentis* – in a position of responsibility – for his slave and is therefore *ipso facto* personally responsible for that slave's actions. Gaius shakes his head decisively. In Rome, slaves are allowed too much latitude for this approach to be practicable. Gaius knows of slaves who run businesses, have slaves of their own and sometimes do not see their masters from one week to the next. In fact, there is an entire body of commercial law stipulating what masters are liable for if a business enterprise run by a slave goes wrong, and what kinds of contracts a slave can sign on his master's behalf without the master even knowing about it. (Gaius looks forward to collating this body of law into a single text – once he finds the time.)

The Praetor strives to look dignified while simultaneously wriggling to relieve the pressure on his numb buttocks. The chair is working as per its specification, and the sooner the Praetor can rise from it, the happier he will be. He mutters a suggestion, and Gaius nods agreement. In fact, the Praetor has come up with the solution Gaius was going to suggest himself, and suitable precedents can be found in the scrolls he carries. However, the jurist senses that a lengthy legal exposition of the matter will not be welcome right now.

He stands back as the Praetor delivers his *praescriptio*. This is the formula – a set of legal points that will be applied to the case when it goes to trial. The jobs of the Praetor in the preliminary work on the case are to appoint a judge, set a date for the actual trial and deliver his formula. The first two items were dealt with while waiting for Gaius, so only the *praescriptio* remains. Even the spectators are hushed as the Praetor makes his announcement.

'It is my ruling, in accordance with the judgement of my predecessors, that in cases such as this no one can act as a proxy. The poisoner chose to kill her victim instead of informing on her master, so the crime is hers alone.' He pauses to let the consequent cheers and catcalls die down.

'However, it is also my judgement that the accused can be charged with *coniuratio* – a criminal conspiracy to poison. Therefore, if it is proven to the jury's satisfaction that the accused was complicit in the crime, either by encouraging its commission, or by procuring the poison, or by providing the poisoner access to the victim, he is an accomplice, deserving of death and the judge shall so rule.'

Hastily, Gaius leans forward and mutters urgently in the Praetor's ear. Even close to, he has to raise his voice to be heard over the wails of the teenage daughters. The Praetor gives Gaius a sour look and signals for silence. 'After consultation, I amend my formula to clarify that it must be proven that if the accused did allow access to the victim, this was done knowingly for the purpose of poisoning. Allowing access without knowledge of the poisoner's intent is not reason to find the accused guilty. Satisfied?'

This last word is muttered out of the side of the Praetor's mouth as he looks at Gaius. The jurist nods absently. He is already gathering his scrolls and preparing to follow in the Praetor's wake as he leaves the crowd and returns gratefully to the letters of Augustus.

The Finding of the *Institutes*

The set of legal opinions compiled by the jurist Gaius was one of the most influential texts of Roman law. This text (called the *Institutes of Gaius*) was eventually replaced by the *Codex of Justinian*, a weighty tome that became the foundation of much of European law. The *Institutes* were presumed to have been lost forever, and the text was indeed lost for fifteen hundred years.

Then, in the early nineteenth century, a scholar was perusing an ancient text of the works of St Jerome in an Italian library. He noted that the text had been written on parchment from which an earlier text had been scrubbed away. Fortunately, under the right lighting this text could be retrieved, and the writings of the jurist Gaius once again saw the light of day.

☷ HORA IV ☷
(10.00 –11.00)

THE TEENAGER BREAKS
UP WITH HER BOYFRIEND

Now I grieve that your foul saliva has polluted the pure lips of a pure girl.

CATULLUS *Carmina* 78b

'Watch where you are going, stupid girl!'

Miyria hardly hears the comment as she crashes into a court official holding an armful of scrolls. She picks herself up and runs on, her attendant clucking to herself as she lifts up the skirts of her *stola* to hurry after her charge.

They were not even meant to be at the court case anyway. Miyria and her attendant were out to select vegetables from the Forum Holitorium when Miyria had impulsively decided to drop in on the case where Cerinthus, the love of her life, would be in attendance with the Praetor. (His name is not really Cerinthus – that's a codename. Cerinthus is actually Marcus Albinus, one of the Praetor's junior clerks. Miyria uses a codename because if her father were to find out about her relationship with the boy, things might go hard for him.)

You cannot believe how strongly the longing for you has overwhelmed me. This longing is almost entirely caused by love, and the fact that we are so seldom apart. Now it happens that I spend most of the night lying awake thinking of you, and in the day my feet take me, unawares, to your room. Of course, you are not there, and I return sad and heartsick, like a rejected lover.

I'm only free of this torture when I have exhausted myself at work, in legal cases and the cases which trouble my friends. So you can imagine what my life is like, when my only solace is in toil, and my only relief the wretchedness and anxieties of others.

PLINY TO CALPURNIA *Letters* 74

Not that there's any longer a chance of that happening. While the Praetor was waiting for some documents or a witness to turn up, Cerinthus had slipped away from his post and into the throng that had gathered around the basilica. Miyria's heart had leapt at the thought that her Cerinthus had seen her and was coming to pass a few stolen moments in her company. As she pushed through the crowd to meet him, Cerinthus was intercepted by a redhead wearing a girl's short, thigh-length dress.

Puzzled, Miyria had stopped, ignoring the tugs at her elbow as her attendant tried to pull her away. Any doubts as to the relationship between Cerinthus and the girl were soon dismissed. Cerinthus gave a quick glance towards the basilica, where the Praetor was deep in consultation with some official, and then pulled the girl behind a pillar for a deep, lascivious kiss, which was heartily reciprocated.

Miyria had no idea how long she stood there, stunned. Eventually, the Praetor left the basilica, and her Cerinthus gave the red-headed girl one last hug and a grope, then hurried after his employer. At that point, half-blinded by tears, Miyria had fled the scene of her betrayal, bumping into the jurist on her way out.

Her home is on the cross street of the road from the Aemilian bridge, not far from the Porticus Octaviae where the hearing was taking place. So within a matter of minutes Miyria had rushed past the startled doorkeeper, fled to her room, flung herself face down on her bed and is now sobbing inconsolably into her pillow. Several minutes later there is a wheezing of breath at the door as the attendant arrives, checks on her charge, and wisely retreats out of the way.

After a while, Miyria composes herself. She has become certain that her relationship with that cheating pig is over – beyond question. Her attendant was right to say that she, the daughter of a wealthy merchant, is far too good for a mere legal clerk. And that he, careless of the risks she had taken, or the fact that she was so willing to ignore their difference in status, had nevertheless so disrespected her – well, that stings almost as much as the betrayal. She knows now that she will never see him again. He will be expecting a message slipped to him during the afternoon by her compliant attendant. Well, let that message be as hurtful as possible – yet also dignified, to show Cerinthus that it is not some street harlot he has lost, but a proper lady.

So far, you aspiring lover, my muse has told you where to seek your prey and how to lay your snares. Now, the woman you have selected must be captivated and held fast. So, seducers everywhere, pay attention to what I now have to say, because this is the most important part of my lesson ...

First of all be certain of this. There is no woman you cannot win if only you are certain that you can win her. The birds would sooner cease to sing in the springtime, the grasshopper would sooner be silent in summer, and a hare turn around and chase the hounds, than a woman be able to resist the sweet wooing of a young lover.

Ovid *Ars amatoria* (The Art of Love)

Fortunately – all unbeknown to Cerinthus – Sulpicia will be her guide, as she was the source of the loving letters she had sent earlier. Sulpicia has been dead now for several generations, but Miyria's most prized possession is a copy of *The Elegies of Tibullus and Propertius*, in which the poems of Sulpicia are preserved. Sulpicia lived in the reign of the emperor Augustus, but she was Miyria's age when she wrote her poetry. Sixteen is late for an aristocratic Roman girl to marry (many are married at the age of thirteen or fourteen), but a merchant's daughter such as Miyria might marry later, at the ripe old age of eighteen. Both girls knew the dark excitement of forbidden romance, and frustration with an older generation which tried to control their every move.

GIRL WEARING A GREEK CHITON PLAYING KNUCKLEBONES.
NOW IN THE BRITISH MUSEUM, LONDON.

ROMANCE (FROM THE PARENT'S POINT OF VIEW)

You have asked me to seek out a husband for your niece... I might have had to search for a long time if Minicius Acilianus were not available... His general appearance is nobly handsome, which is a point that should not be overlooked, for a girl should get someone good-looking in exchange for her virginity.

Since it is you for whom we are seeking a son-in-law, I should probably not mention anything about money, but anyone else would want to know that he is extremely wealthy... If you want to think of the well-being of your children and their descendants, then actually anyone seeking a husband should take this into account.

PLINY TO JUNIUS MAURICUS *Letters* 1,14

'*Hic animum sensusque meos abducta relinquo, arbitrio quamvis non sinis esse meo!*' (He knows how I feel about this abduction, yet ignores the will of my heart!)[6] When Miyria read this bitter protest about being taken from Rome on her birthday, and so away from her sweetheart, she immediately identified with a girl who, like herself, has constant constraints on where she cannot or must go, and whom she sees or cannot see.

A hot blush creeps up her cheeks as she remembers the last letter to Cerinthus, lifted entirely from the writing of Sulpicia. Yet not really dishonestly so. It was just that Sulpicia had been able to say what she wanted to say better than she had been able to say it herself (Sulpicia 6):

> *My light, perhaps you don't love me,*
> *The way I think you did a few days ago,*
> *If ever in my young life,*
> *I have ever done anything as stupid,*
> *As leaving you there alone –*
> *Know that this was done,*
> *To hide my ardent lust.*

The next letter Miyria had planned to send – as soon as her father's travels had taken him out of the Rome, and her scandalized attendant could be persuaded to look the other way – was to have been modelled on the first of Sulpicia's poems:

> *Venus has kept her promises*
> *And brought my love to my heart*
> *Let my story of happiness be revealed*

To those who feel I have missed my share
Must I pass this letter to someone
Who will touch it before he does himself?
But there's another kind of shame
When you fit your face to your reputation.
So let this be said to all ...

With tears running down her face, Miyria whispers to herself the long-memorized last line: *cum digno, digna fuisse ferar* – with a worthy man, I have been a worthy woman.

She'd had it all planned. With the consummation of their love, she and Cerinthus would unofficially be a couple. Her father would certainly erupt when she told him the news, but Miyria has always been able to twist him around her finger. He would come round when he saw that their love was real, and how happy it made his daughter.

⸻

Let us live, my Lesbia, and let us love!
And not give a penny for
the scandalized mutterings of stern old men.
The sun, once set, will rise again
But we, when our brief day is over
Sleep in everlasting night.

CATULLUS *Carmina* 5

⸻

Then the relationship would no longer be a secret: Cerinthus would become Marcus Albinus, and when the two were married, he would leave the Praetor's employ. He would take his place in her father's business as his son-in-law and potential successor. All this, all their future life together, Cerinthus has thrown away for some red-headed hussy!

Carefully, Miyria picks up the *libellus* that she had secreted into her room yesterday afternoon. Now, instead of the warm, longing message that it would have carried to her love, the message will be cold, distant – and final. The *libellus* itself comprises two thin boards of wood pierced twice on one side and bound together with twine. The inner side of each board is coated with a layer of wax, and Miyria will use her sharp-pointed stylus to scratch her message into the wax. Indeed, because she has written her love notes on the wax, it is that wax – *cerinthus* in Latin – which has become Albinus' codename. (Another idea stolen from Sulpicia.)

Albinus is actually the kind of semi-literate lout who would never read poetry for pleasure (how clear his faults now seem!), so there is no harm in lifting the entire message straight from the verses of Sulpicia. Her dismissal of her boyfriend was refined and dignified, yet hurtful – exactly as Miyria wants hers to be. She begins by digging the stylus so deeply into the wax that it scores the wood behind. That will never do. It shows her emotions are out of control. Heating a flat, round-bladed knife blade over a candle, she then smooths the wax and starts again:

Well, thank you for showing me that you are a cheat,
As it has prevented me from making a fool of myself
That tart probably wove her own flashy toga
She whom you prefer to
Miyria, daughter of Miyrius of Mari.
(They were a bit worried about me,
Lest I marry a social inferior.)

Miyria re-reads the lines. It is, of course, Sulpicia's fourth poem to the letter, except where she has substituted 'Miyria, daughter of Miyrius of Mari' for the original line, 'Sulpicia, daughter of the Servi'. It's a pity, because the original *Sulpicia Servi Filia* carries the inscriptional weight and grandeur of centuries of nobility. It's something you simply can't carry off if you are a pepper trader's daughter. On the other hand, the previous lines are wonderfully catty, implying that Cerinthus' *amatorix*, his woman on the side, is not just working class but a prostitute (they being the only women in Rome who wear togas).

Overall, Miyria feels a certain grim satisfaction as she uses the ends of the twine to bind the two boards together. She imagines Albinus' smug pleasure at receiving what he imagines to be another sweet message from his little dupe, and then his horror and despair as he realizes that he has lost her, finally and forever.

Then Miyria remembers that just as Albinus has lost her, so too she has lost him. She throws herself at her pillow, and the tears begin again.

⚏ HORA V ⚏
(11.00–12.00)

THE STONEMASON WORKS ON AN IMPERIAL TOMB

Rome extends its labours into the fifth hour.

MARTIAL, *Satires* 4.8.3

His business has taken the Praetor to the Campus Martius, and so to Rome's exercise and recreational area goes Miyria's attendant, bearing her final message for the young man in the Praetor's entourage.

As she makes her way through the crowded streets, the attendant reflects on how the area for exercise and recreation has shrunk considerably since the days of the Republic. Where once there were open fields, now the space is packed with monuments, buildings, tombs and temples. Here, for example, is rising the splendid dome of what will be one of the emperor Hadrian's lasting gifts to his city – the rebuilt Pantheon, temple to all the Olympian gods.

THE CAMPUS MARTIUS IN EARLIER TIMES

There were never more zealous builders than Pompey, the Divine [Julius] Caesar, and Augustus' friends … The Campus Martius is where most of these buildings are situated, and the foresight with which these buildings were planned has resulted in their augmenting the natural beauty of the place.

The Campus is remarkably large, as indeed chariot races can be staged at the same time as equestrian events, while the rest of the populace entertain themselves by rolling hoops, playing ball and wrestling, for grass covers the entire area all of the year.

This, and the works of art situated about hilltops above the river sloping down to its bed, all resembles the painted backdrop at a theatre, a spectacle which captures and holds the eye.

STRABO, *Geography* 5.3.8

Over the River Tiber, an even more impressive, barrel-shaped structure is looming. This is not a temple, but a tomb. Hadrian will one day be dead and buried, but the monumental edifice in which he will be interred ensures that he will never be forgotten. The attendant looks at the tiny figure of a stonemason working on one of the many statues atop the tomb, and reflects that with all this building going on, this is a good time to be an artisan in Rome.

Postumus Gallienus, master stonemason, would agree – though he might also mutter into his beard that it is possible for a man to have too much of a good thing. His skills are much in demand, with 'demand' being the operative word. Gallienus has a reputation as the man who can handle a tricky crafting job. When the marble starts showing hairline cracks, when a particularly fissile block of limestone threatens to crumble at the touch of a chisel, when a careless whack of a hammer has inadvertently and treasonously removed the nose from the emperor's statue – that's when the great and good of Rome send out messengers urgently demanding the presence of Postumus Gallienus to put things right.

Gallienus sometimes wonders if it was overwork that killed his father. As the name 'Postumus'[7] indicates, Gallienus senior died while his wife was pregnant with his unborn son. The stonemason's yard he left behind was carefully curated by an uncle until that son, Gallienus, had come of age. That same uncle had also taught Gallienus the family craft of stone-working, before he himself died in a building site accident. (That was when Hadrian's predecessor Trajan was extending the Circus Maximus so that even more spectators could watch the chariot races. The splendid white marble seats at the refurbished racetrack are, Gallienus believes, a fitting monument to his beloved uncle.)

Though only in his early forties, in the few idle moments of each busy day Gallienus himself sometimes thinks about retirement. Certainly, he is wealthy enough, but despite being twice married and twice widowed he has no child to whom he can leave his thriving business. And it would be a pity to simply abandon the firm that has been so carefully built up over two generations. Also, retirement is rare among working-class Romans, most of whom simply work until they drop. However, the main thing keeping Gallienus from downing tools and going to live on a quiet farm in the country is something quite different.

Being a master stonemason is not just what Gallienus does, it's what he is. If he's not stretching his skills on a difficult bit of stone, or consulting on a tricky engineering job, he does not feel properly alive. Working with stone – comfortable, amenable travertine; rugged, unpredictable granite; noble marble in its many colours – this is what he lives for. Giving it up to watch cows defecate in some rural field would be more of a nightmare than dream ending to his days.

At the moment, Gallienus is on a monumental run. Quite literally, he has been running from one monument to another for the entire month. There's another month's worth of work backlogged at the current site alone. Hadrian's planned mausoleum is a massive edifice 48 metres high and with a garden on the roof. This garden is 64 metres across and is strewn with statues of men and horses. Later, a colossal statue depicting the emperor driving a four-horse chariot (*quadriga*) will be added to the top of the entire structure.

The Original Mausoleum

The term 'mausoleum' comes from a name – that of Mausolus of Halicarnassus. This king (who ruled the same city in Asia Minor that was once the home of the historian Herodotus) was buried in a monument of such grandeur that it became one of the seven wonders of the ancient world. Ever since, any burial place constructed on an ambitious scale has been known as a 'mausoleum'.

Gallienus is there to repair and re-head one of these statues. This particular statue was originally a marble depiction of some mid-Republican nobody. It had been on the site when the builders arrived, and was removed and stored to be later re-purposed. Like most 'portrait' statues, it had been made in two separate parts: body and head. Gallienus has a number of similar statues in his yard. They depict generic young bodies in military gear, in athletic poses or bathing.

It works like this: assume someone wants a statue of him- (or her-) self. The person to be portrayed will go to a sculptor who will make a lifelike head, the neck of which will finish with a standard-sized stone wedge. The subject of the statue will then take that head and visit a number of stonemasons' yards like Gallienus', until he or she finds a body in a pleasing and compatible form and pose.

The bodies all come with standard-sized sockets for these head-wedges, so the stonemason is able to seamlessly unite body and head into a single statue, ready for placement in a garden, country villa or wherever. This system has the disadvantage that, for example, one occasionally comes across the head of a mature Roman matron frowning severely above the bathing body of a barely post-pubescent Venus. On the other hand, it has the advantage that as soon as the aforesaid matron has passed away, her head can be whipped off and replaced, more appropriately, with one of her granddaughter's. (Note, incidentally, that re-heading the statue of a living emperor in this way is treason, and may lead to the head of the perpetrator being removed in a non-replaceable manner.)

In this particular case, the Republican nobody evidently had clear objections to being replaced by posterity, for his head has been very firmly fixed into place. So firmly, in fact, that in the process of removing the head an inexperienced workman had caused the entire torso to crack diagonally across and deposit on the ground a pile of rubble consisting of one arm, half a chest and a good bit of abdomen. Gallienus has spent the last two days putting everything back together. He has noted that even if the subject had been a nobody, he was evidently a rich nobody, for the entire statue is of fine Parian marble, which is why the builders want to keep it.

Gallienus drills a hole at forty-five degrees and half a thumb's length wide into the standing part of the torso, and then a matching hole into the separated lump. Then he slots an iron bar into the hole, and smears fine concrete made with marble dust over the parts where the two pieces are joined. Carefully sanded and painted over (the Romans paint their statues to make them more lifelike) no one will see the join.

In working with stone, Gallienus often also works with both concrete and cement. He is contemptuous of those who do not know the difference between these two materials. The cement comes from ash deposited in an ancient volcanic flow mined from the Alban hills (the emperor Augustus, impressed by the quality of this material, decreed that this alone should be used for monumental government

A STONEMASON WITH HIS TOOLS.
MUSÉE D'AQUITAINE, BORDEAUX

structures in Rome). The cement is mixed with crushed stone or aggregate to make concrete. Many impressive Roman structures, such as the Flavian Amphitheatre some call the Colosseum, are actually made of this concrete. Thus, Gallienus is often called on to help decide the best way to hang a stone frontage on to these concrete buildings, so that they seem to have been made of stone throughout.

Once he has finished with this statue, Gallienus will need to gather his crew and rush to his next job. This is also an imperial mausoleum – the mausoleum of Augustus, which, from his vantage point atop Hadrian's future tomb, Gallienus can see across the Campus Martius. In a way, the two mausoleums are actually linked. Augustus had his tomb built not just for himself, but also for his family. Then because every subsequent emperor claimed, however speciously, to be a Caesar and therefore a scion of the imperial house, many of them – and their wives and mothers – had been interred in that same mausoleum. Which was now so packed with deceased emperors and their relations that it was running out of room. (The emperor Vespasian and his dynasty chose to be buried elsewhere, but the tomb was re-opened for the late emperor Nerva.)

Then Hadrian's predecessor Trajan had solved the problem of post-mortem overcrowding – in his own case, at least – by being interred at the base of a monumental column, up which spiralled carved images of his victories in the Dacian War (the young Gallienus had worked on some of the bas-reliefs). However, Hadrian had correctly discerned that if every emperor followed Trajan's precedent, Rome would quickly become forested with monumental columns. Therefore, he had set about building an imperial tomb capable of holding all the dead emperors of the foreseeable future – plagues, assassinations and civil wars notwithstanding.

Hadrian had prepared his tomb at the riverside close to the Aelian bridge. He was buried there, for the Mausoleum of Augustus was full and thenceforth no one else was interred there.

CASSIUS DIO *History* 49.23.1

Though now removed from active service, this does not mean that the tomb of Augustus can be left rot in peace. Apart from the need to show respect for the imperial dead, decay of the imperial tomb is a terrible omen for the sitting emperor. When a large crack once appeared in the tomb of Augustus a century ago, it was widely interpreted as foretelling the death of the then emperor Vespasian (and foretelling it correctly, as things turned out). The fact that its neglect can be a harbinger of doom would alone be reason enough for emperors to be obsessive about keeping the tomb in tip-top shape, but the fact is that Augustus' mausoleum is also regarded as a fine civic monument in its own right.

Although, at 42 metres (the bronze statue of Augustus that tops the edifice is almost at the height of Hadrian's mausoleum) the structure looks almost natural, with its concentric rings of earth. Especially as the whole thing is planted with evergreen trees and resembles a peaceful hillock as much as a man-made construction. In fact, the overall structure is slightly larger than Hadrian's monument, because as an emperor, Hadrian is too tactful to build a mausoleum bigger than that of his great predecessor. However, Augustus' mausoleum deliberately blends into and becomes part of the scenery. Hadrian's building, looming over the Tiber as it does, is a deliberately more in-your-face type of structure that seems even larger than it actually is.

The most remarkable of these tombs is the one they call the Mausoleum. It is a lofty, massive mound near the river. The foundation is white marble, and the whole is thickly covered with evergreen trees to the very top. There on top is a bronze statue of Augustus Caesar standing above the mortal remains of his family and friends.

Behind this are the marvellous promenades of a large tholos [sacred precinct] of white marble with wonderful promenades. … The wall is surrounded by a circular iron fence and the ground within is thick with black poplars.

CASSIUS DIO *History* 49.23.1

In front of Augustus' tomb is the *horologium*, one of the first Egyptian obelisks ever brought to Rome. This is one of Gallienus' favourite structures, for when he passes it on a sunny day a quick glance at the pavement in front of the obelisk tells him the time of day and even the season. In fact, there is a line marked on the stone flags north of the obelisk that shows the maximum stretch of the shadow at different times of the year.

Detractors say that the whole thing was designed only so that on Augustus' birthday the shadow of the obelisk would point directly at the door to Augustus' tomb, but the sceptical Gallienus doubts that the whole thing is merely a propaganda exercise. Rather, the obelisk, by measuring the length of the shadow cast by the sun, acts as physical proof that the calendar reformed by Julius Caesar (and refined later) is truly keeping track of the seasons. In the last days of the Republic, the calendar was so wildly out of sync with reality that summer festivals were sometimes celebrated in ankle-deep snow.

Today, Gallienus will be visiting the mausoleum at the order of a high imperial official. Two plain obelisks from Egypt flank the entrance to the tomb, and its caretakers have reported that a type of fungus seems to be spreading across the back of each. Gallienus will inspect the infestation, and advise on how the rare red granite can be best cleaned without any damage that would also give the fungus an even better footing in the future. While he is at it, the official's clerk mentioned, some of the marble stone on the lower wall could use some re-pointing. Overall, a couple of hours' work, and send the bill to the Palatine as usual.

Well, the *horologium* is doing its job today. From his vantage point Gallienus can see that the tip of the shadow rests right on the point of his lunchtime. Gathering his tools, the stonemason swings them in a sack on to his shoulder and shouts to his assistants that it's time to knock off for the morning.

⚏ HORA VI ⚏
(12.00–13.00)

THE TAVERN KEEPER
AT LUNCHTIME

The first tavern in a dark street swallowed the girls, in their loose dresses and dishevelled hair.

PROPERTIUS *Love Elegies* 4.8

The stonemason stops in front of the Ninth Pillar tavern, and halts so abruptly that a passer-by on the street jostles him. The stranger is about to make an angry comment but stops himself, and hurries of instead – years of handling large blocks of stone have given the mason biceps that bulge intimidatingly.

'What gives, Copa?' Gallienus asks, as he makes his way in past the woman in front of him. (Everyone calls her Copa, though her name is actually Myrtalis. 'Copa' is simply the feminine of the word for 'tavern owner', but Myrtalis has owned the place for so long now that she herself occasionally forgets her given name.)

At present, Copa is leaning across the doors of her inn, scrubbing and cursing furiously. Closer examination shows that some vandal has decorated the doors with a variety of penises drawn in charcoal. Copa pauses and pushes a sweat-soaked wisp of dark-blonde hair from her forehead. The graffiti is vindictiveness, she explains, on the part of a customer who got thrown out last night.

'He ignored the sign,' she remarks, jerking her thumb at the interior of the tavern. Though it can't be seen from the sunlit street, there's a fresco painted on the wall of the tavern's main room. The painting shows a young man furiously kissing a young slave girl, who wears a voluminous yellow dress and is doing her best to fight off her evidently unwelcome suitor. The inscription below reads '*Nolo cvm Syrisca*' ('No [messing] with Syrisca'). The name has changed several times over the past few years – tavern girls, even those who are slaves, tend to find other employment as soon as they are able.

'The problem with these cheap alleyway adulterers,' remarks Copa, 'is that they all think everyone is getting it off with the serving girls except them. This drunken sot gave the tavern a lecture about stealing 'his' girl. There were a bunch of Celtiberians in the place last night, and he informed them that they were a bunch of hairy fools who live in Spanish rabbit burrows and clean their teeth with urine [admittedly, they actually do that last one]. Then he offered to take on the lot of them. It did not end well. But I wouldn't have to tell you that if you know anything about Celtiberians.' She nods at the crude drawings. 'Then these pictures showed up. He must have come back here before dawn, but I only noticed when I opened for lunch.'[8]

Assorted nuts [...] drinks: 14 as; lard: 2 as; bread: 3 as; three cuts of meat: 12 as; four sausages: 8 as. Overall: 51 as.

BAR BILL FOUND AT HERCULANEUM *Corpus Inscriptionum Latinarum* 4 n10674

Copa lives in her own tavern. Because the place is usually open until midnight – and sometimes later, if the aediles are in a forgiving mood – hers is not one of those establishments open for breakfast. However, it's worth waiting for lunch here, because the Ninth Pillar is one of the most attractive eateries on the lower Esquiline. The wine actually tastes of grapes, rather than the usual offerings hereabouts that taste as though the proprietors brewed it in their boots (as the saying goes). However, chief of the attractions of the Ninth Pillar Tavern is the attractive Syrisca.

Copa herself is best described as 'beefy'. This attribute is on occasion useful, since when Syrisca dances for the customers, her face flushed with wine and a Grecian headband in her hair, the customers definitely pay attention. Even those on the expensive couches in the alcove at the back – with rose-petal garlands on their heads and whom Copa intends to ply with wine until the sunset – will sit up and pay attention. But their eyes are all that they will lay on the girl. There's a hickory stick by Copa's elbow that's almost as thick as her wrist. Anyone who attempts to shift Syrisca's dancing from the vertical to the horizontal gets acquainted with the hickory shortly before being ejected at medium velocity from the premises.

COPA'S SONG

Syrisca is dancing, drunkenly, sensuously,
A Greek headband in her hair
Gyrating her hips in practised rhythm
To her castanets …
How does it help a weary man
To be off in the hot dust of day
Rather than to lie back here …
drinking from readily refilled cups?
Come rest your tired body
Under the shadowing vines
With a garland of roses crowning your head
As you snatch a kiss from the sweet lips
Of a youthful girl.

PSEUDO-VERGIL *Copa* (passim)

The customers are not entirely to blame. Many a Roman drinking house (*popina*) also serves as a brothel (*lupanaria*), just as other taverns also serve as inns or boarding houses, or combine all of these services. Many taverngoers automatically assume that the tavern girls are available, but that's not the case at the Ninth Pillar. Copa has no moral objections to prostituting her barmaids, it's just that it's wearisome sorting out fights between jealous customers on the one hand and jealous bar girls on the other, and it is downright annoying to lose good staff to pregnancy. So Copa keeps it clean – not out of morality, but for convenience.

Her work outside done, Copa makes her way back into the friendly shadows of her establishment. There's a fug of wood smoke from the cooking fires; the aroma of freshly baked bread mingles with the smell of the roasting ducks and asparagus that will make up today's main course. There's also the lingering fragrance of the applewood that Copa burns every morning to hide the sour stink of old wine and close-packed and poorly bathed humanity that is an inescapable part of every tavern's atmosphere.

There's also a positive racket of conversation. Syrisca isn't dancing right now (because the tavern is packed with customers), and though the patrons appreciate the show, they appreciate a good meal even more. For many of those present, the sixth hour marks the end of the working day, which began an hour before dawn. The plan now is to eat a square meal, wash it down with several beakers of watered wine, and head home to sleep before joining friends at dinner.

Consequently, Syrisca and two other serving girls are moving about busily carrying laden platters between the benches, amiably swatting away groping hands and exchanging low-quality witticisms and greetings with regular customers. There's a reason that coarse pick-up lines are called *taberna blandita*, for the mildly intoxicated patrons of the Ninth Pillar are as incapable of coming up with finely honed Latin epigram as the recipients are of appreciating them. Taverns have the reputation of being rather crude, earthy places, and the Ninth Pillar does its best to live down to that reputation.

←—————————————————————————→

THE POET FLORUS TO HADRIAN

I wouldn't want to be Caesar,
And tramp round Britain,
Getting ague in my knees
For Scythian frosts later to freeze.

HADRIAN'S REPLY

I wouldn't want to be Florus
And lurk in pubs,
Eating pies and peas
And wander round wine-shops
Getting infested with fleas.

HISTORIA AUGUSTA *Hadrian* 16

←————————————————————————→

Even the duck being served for lunch is pushing the envelope of the law. The prudish emperor Tiberius forbade the selling of any food at establishments where drink was also sold, though the emperor Nero (himself a connoisseur of low dives) allowed cooked beans and other vegetables to be served. Technically speaking, those laws are still in place and can be enforced if the authorities are paid to take an interest. As a result, Copa makes sure she stays on good terms with her competition, the takeaway joint further up the street near the temple of Castor and Pollux. (Though she also occasionally requests some of the rougher elements of her clientele to drop broad hints to the takeaway's ownership of what might happen should those good terms ever worsen.)

As Copa pushes through the throng, pausing to chat with favoured customers, her alert ears pick up a distinctive rattling sound over the general hubbub. She changes direction, pushing patrons aside like a grain tanker moving through a choppy sea. Two gamblers are peering intently at five dice on the table, which lie beside the leather cup from which they were thrown. 'That's a two,' insists one, squinting in the poor light at the worn spots in the dice. 'A three,' insists his companion, and the pair might have come to blows had not each been seized firmly about the neck by one of Copa's meaty hands.

'Are you trying to get my licence revoked?' growls the infuriated innkeeper, 'Or do you think this is the Saturnalia?' (The Saturnalia – Rome's winter festival – is the only time that gambling is allowed in public places.) The men grin sheepishly, while those about offer loud advice as to what Copa might do with the offending dice. Diplomatically ignoring the hecklers, Copa sweeps the dice into their cup and tucks it into her robe. 'Get them when you leave,' she tells the gamblers. Judging by their coarse, hooded cloaks, the pair are freedmen, and not well off. Permanent confiscation of the dice would not just be a financial blow, but it would also lose her a pair of regular customers.

Copa puts the leather cup with the dice on a shelf in the kitchen. This is a small, unpleasantly hot room that leads to the alley out back, which – despite punishments and protestations – often serves as a toilet of first resort for the tavern's more desperate customers.

Copa remembers a drunken crowd that pushed through the kitchen en route to the alley last week. One managed to set himself on fire when he brushed too closely to the oven where some scrawny thrushes were roasting. There was pandemonium, with fire and flaming guests appearing randomly in the crowded room while the staff battled to put out the blaze and other opportunistic intruders tried to grab the food. Sometimes, Copa wishes she were a man and could try a more relaxing career – perhaps a legionary post on the Rhine fighting off Germanic raiders.

Talking of raiders … Copa ducks out into the small walled yard at the back and checks that no one has sneaked through to steal one of the earthen *amphorae* stacked against the back wall. These *amphorae* contain the tavern's reserve of wine. Every few hours, Copa will herself take one of these tall jugs, whack out the stopper and pour the contents into something between a small barrel and a huge jug. It is from this vessel that wine is dispensed to the customers, and it bears the encouraging inscription '*Qvi vult, svmat Ocane, veni bibe*' ('I am the Ocean, let he who wants come and drink').

DANCING GIRL WITH GREEK-STYLE CLOTHING AND FLORAL WREATH.

Sextilanus, you are getting as drunk as a lord (or five)
You'd be drunk on water too if you'd drunk that much of it
You haven't just scrounged drinking money off those nearby
But people sitting on distant benches.
This isn't plonk from a Pelignian press
Or cheap wine from the Tuscan hills
It's Massic wine in age-dark casks
From the time of Opimius.
Tell the tavern keeper to bring you
The dregs of his Laletan casks, Sextilanus
If you are going to drink more than ten beakers.

MARTIAL *Epigrams* 1.26

A sudden increase in the roar of voices from the main room alerts Copa to yet more trouble. There's a crowd gathered around one of the tables, and a furious Syrisca trying to hit someone through the throng. Persuaded by Copa's hickory stick, the crowd parts to reveal two men savagely wrestling on one of the benches, spreading a meal of lentils and red beans across the wooden surface as they do so. This is no unusual occurrence – in fact, it is so usual that there's a valedictory notice over the door, which Copa points out to the lightly stunned combatants before she hurls them physically into the street: *ITIS FORAS RIXATIS* (Do your fighting outside).

Within the tavern, the patrons have already settled back to their meal. Copa thoughtfully sucks a forefinger that had got caught between the two heads she has just violently banged together, and decides that the main lunchtime rush is over. The girls can take it from here. She wants to sneak out to see about a special birthday gift she is arranging for her father.

Successus, the weaver, loves Iris, the innkeeper's slave girl. Even though she does not love him, he begs her to have pity.

[In another hand] Go away.

Successus: Why so jealous and getting in the way? Stand aside for a younger, more handsome fellow who is being very badly treated.

[Reply] That's my verdict. I've written all there is to say. You might love Iris. She doesn't love you.

Corpus Inscriptionum Latinarum 4, 1.10.2–3 (Bar of Prima); 8258, 8259[9]

⚏ HORA VII ⚏
(13.00–14.00)

THE WATER-CLOCKMAKER
STARTS A PROJECT

*May the gods destroy the man who first found out how to
distinguish hours … to hack my wretched days into small chunks.*

Roman Playwright **PLAUTUS,** *quoted in Aulus Gellius NA* 3.3.1

Copa wants to give a clock to her father because, like most Romans, he
rather enjoys a post-prandial nap. Then *pater* heads down to the baths
for a game of ball with his elderly cronies. (The Roman version of the
game is a lively cross between handball and murderball.) The problem
is getting the entire group together for a synchronized start, for, as the
proverb goes: 'Sooner two clocks will agree than two philosophers',
with the implication that both groups tend to be rather idiosyncratic.
Just to make things more complex, Copa's dad is a heavy sleeper, who

often snores on well past the hour that he has allocated for exercise, and wakes up, grumpy and irritable, in time for supper. What he needs is an alarm clock.

As it happens, alarm clocks are a relatively simple proposition. One of the most basic of these was invented centuries ago by Ctesibius of Alexandria. It works like this: you take a jug and fill it with water according to the allocated time marked on the inside. This is then poured into a reservoir, from which water flows at a fixed rate. When the amount of water in the reservoir gets below a certain weight, a built-in scale tips a finely sanded lead ball into a vertical tube. The tube is the exact diameter of the ball, so as the ball falls it pushes air out through a whistle fixed to the bottom. The result is a piercing shriek at exactly the prescribed time after the water was poured.

In the modern era the sixth hour (*hora sexta*) survives, though it has drifted across the dial to become the *siesta*, the time for an afternoon nap. At some point in history it swapped places with the ninth hour (*hora nona*), which has become 'noon'.

For many Romans (apart from aficionados of the springtime orgies of the Festival of Flora) the best time of the year was the midwinter Saturnalia holiday. It was a cruel irony that just when the partying, gift-giving and merriment were at their height, the hours were at their shortest. Time really did fly when one was having fun.

This is the basis of the *clepsydra* – the water thief, as this type of clock is called in the timekeeping trade, though most Romans simply call it the *horologium ex aqua* (the clock from water). The basic alarm clock variety can be found in numerous situations. For example, in courts it measures the amount of time allocated to each speaker. In brothels the punters have to beat the clock. In both cases, a little ball of wax is kept handy with which to bung up the water outflow if the proceedings are interrupted for any reason.

Since it does not depend on the observation of the sometimes overcast skies, the water clock is the most reliable way of keeping time. As a result of this dependability, it was first used by the Egyptians for a few hundred years before they passed it on to the Greeks, who passed it on to the Romans, with each nation adding various refinements along the way. A fully fledged water clock is a wonder of engineering, and does much more than shriek, bong or clang at the end of an hour. It has to be complex because keeping time over a longer period is a tricky business.

Tricky? Water flows out of a container at a fixed rate. Once you have measured out an hour, multiply the amount of water by twenty-four and you have a day – what's hard about that? Well, start with variable pressure. The more water there is in a container, the more pressure there is at the bottom, and the water spurts out faster. So, midnight to 1 a.m. would go faster than 11 p.m. to midnight. (In fact this is a minor issue, easily dealt with by having a second reservoir that keeps the timekeeping reservoir topped up to a constant level.)

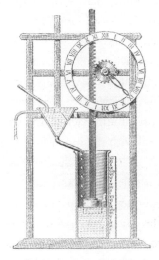

ROMAN WATER-CLOCK DESIGN

No, the real problem lies in the nature of Roman days and nights. Each lasts for twelve hours, from sunup to sundown, and from sundown to dawn. This would be fine, if only every day were the spring and autumn equinox, when day and night are exactly the same length. However, a day at midsummer is a great deal longer than a day in midwinter, though each is still exactly twelve Roman hours long. To keep with twelve hours for each day and night, Roman hours get longer and shorter with the seasons. This means that sundials work perfectly all year long, but variable hours present the clockmaker with a major challenge.

For example, at the equinox, the time taken to get through this hour, *hora septima*, is just under three-quarters the time it will take at the summer solstice, but a quarter longer than it did at the midwinter festival. Once you have calibrated for the shorter or longer day, you need to build in a mirror system to measure the nights, which are doing the opposite. Nor do the days move smoothly across this half-hour variation in the annual length of the Roman hour. Winter hours remain short until the spring, after which they start to lengthen rapidly. The philosopher Aristarchus of Samos (circa 300 BC) would argue that this is because the Earth has an oval orbit around the Sun, but the man was evidently a fool and his argument was comprehensively shot down by Archimedes. The current approach to the issue skips the theorizing and attempts to deal with the inconvenient reality.

Every clockmaker has his own approach to the problem of variable hours and to almost every other aspect of clockmaking. (Sooner do two clock-makers agree …?) For instance, Albinus, the clockmaker who is making the clock for Copa's father, belongs to the inflow school. That is, his devices measure time by the amount of water that has flowed into a container. This sets Albinus' timepieces apart from those of what he calls 'clumsy pesudo-mechanics', which use the outflow system to measure time by the amount that has drained from a container. In reality, both systems have advantages and disadvantages for displaying time, and both types of clock are widely used, insofar as either is used at all. Most people find squinting at the sun and agreeing the time by consensus works just fine.

This is one reason that water clocks are rare. There is little point in being the only man in the neighbourhood who knows the exact time. However, a water clock is not simply a timepiece. The workmanship and engineering involved mean that the owner of such a clock is a gentleman of prestige among his peers, for he can afford so elegant a luxury. It means, for example, that owning the definitive timepiece will allow Copa's father to become the arbiter of who in his ball-playing group is early or late for their afternoon sessions. It is such specific requirements that mean that the construction of each water clock involves detailed consultations between Albinus and his client to determine the exact purpose of the clock, and therefore the type of bells and whistles – literally – that he should build in.

A good dinner was promised. … One of Agamemnon's servants came up as we stood hesitating, and said, 'Do you not know at whose house it is today? Trimalchio, a very rich man, who has a clock in his dining room, and a uniformed trumpeter who keeps telling him how much of his life is lost and gone.'

PETRONIUS *Satyricon* 26

Copa has pretty much settled on giving her father a dial clock. This beast is the size of a wardrobe, and has the time showing in a cylinder built into the middle. Every day at dawn the clock chimes gently, reminding the owner to rotate the dial built into the base by one notch. There are 366 holes drilled around the edge of the dial, each slightly smaller than the next. Rotating the dial clockwise from midwinter to midsummer allows less water to flow into the measuring drum, and so it takes correspondingly longer for each hour to fill. Rotate anti-clockwise, and by midwinter the water positively gushes into the measure, making the short daylight hours pass in no time. That's the use of 183 of the holes. The corresponding holes on the other side of the dial measure the night hours, and though they might be much larger or smaller than the holes opposite, the combined diameter of the two holes is always the same.

Apart from a dial clock, another option discussed at length between Copa and Albinus was the cone clock. This is used for municipal clocks where low maintenance is more important than the amount of space the machine takes up. A cone placed in a large reservoir means that there is lots of water to fill up a measure of a winter day, but by the dog days of summer, when the water level has reached the base of the cone, the cone takes up most of the tank and there is only a miserable trickle to measure away the slow hours.

Another solution to the varying length of the hours is described by the writer Vitruvius in his *De Architectura*, written almost a century previously.

> *Inside, behind the face of the dial, place a reservoir, and let the*
> *water run down into it through a pipe, and let it have a hole*

at the bottom. *Fastened to it is a bronze drum with an opening through which the water flows into it from the reservoir. Enclosed in this drum there is a smaller one, the two being perfectly jointed together by tenon and socket, in such a way that the smaller drum revolves closely but easily in the larger, like a stopcock.*

Hence, when the sun is in Capricornus, the tongue on the rim touches every day one of the points in Capricornus on the lip of the larger drum, and is perpendicular to the strong pressure of the running water. So the water is quickly driven through the opening in the rim to the inside of the vessel, which, receiving it and soon becoming full, shortens and diminishes the length of the days and hours. But when, owing to the daily revolution of the smaller drum, its tongue reaches the points in Aquarius, the opening will no longer be perpendicular, and the water must give up its vigorous flow and run in a slower stream. Thus, the less the velocity with which the vessel receives the water, the more the length of the days is increased.

Then there is this clock that is more like the clocks in millennia to come.

A regular flow of water through the orifice raises an inverted bowl, called by mechanicians the 'cork' or 'drum'. To this are attached a rack and a revolving drum, both fitted with teeth at regular intervals. These teeth, acting upon one another, induce a measured revolution and movement. Other racks and other drums, similarly toothed and subject to the same motion, give rise by their revolution to various kinds of motions, by which figures are moved, cones revolve, pebbles or eggs fall, trumpets sound, and other incidental effects take place. The hours are marked in these

clocks on a column or a pilaster, and a figure emerging from the
bottom points to them with a rod throughout the whole day.

Vitruvius *De Architectura*, 9.8.6–13 passim (trans. Oxford University Press 1914)

Albinus does not have a large working yard, as might a stonemason or builder. While these other craftsmen do their business on a larger scale, it is rare for Albinus to have more than two clocks on the go at any one time. Usually, one of these will be a more expensive model – in this case, a small but precise portable clock by which a physician might time the pulse of a patient's heartbeat – and the other will be a cruder device. This latter model is being made by Albinus' trainee – an enterprising freedman from Asia Minor to whom Albinus intends to sell the business when he is ready to retire. This clock is being made as much to train the freedman as it is for profit.

Albinus' 'yard' (such as it is) is a cleared garden space now occupied by a sundial with the markings drawn to the most exacting standards. Here, a slave has the job of standing by a newly completed water clock as it runs and carefully marking the hour on the clock's cylinder to ensure that sundial and water clock are in complete agreement. It is sometimes necessary to recalibrate a clock. For example, if the owner moves significantly further north or south – say to Gaul or Sicily – then the length of the daytime and nighttime hours will be at variance with the hours in Rome and water outflows will have to be painstakingly adjusted to fit the local conditions. Albinus rather envies his contemporaries who live on the equator – if there are any such – since for them every day and night is exactly twelve hours long with no fluctuations. What a simple job timekeeping must be in such places!

A Roman traveller with a sundial would find that in Rome the shadow that was eight-ninths the length of the gnomon (the spike which cast the shadow) was three-quarters the length in Athens and only three-fifths the length in Alexandria.

The clockmaker tries to persuade Copa that she should also buy her father an elaborate device that moves a needle through a map of the constellations, and so keeps track of the seasons by careful usage of gears and levers. However, the shrewd innkeeper is having none of it. Such devices are useful for astronomers, she allows, but these people also insist on a twenty-four-hour day with hours of fixed length so as to standardize their measurements. However, Copa wants a real clock for her father, who will use it for practical purposes. If she wants to know the season she'll look at the night sky or the state of the leaves on the plane tree in her yard.

A thought strikes her. By all means build the dial, she tells Albinus, as it will impress the grey-beards of her father's group. But leave out the complex machinery behind it. She will just remind her father's slave to advance the needle a bit further every week.

'What matters it in what part of the great theatre he sits when he can scarce hear the horns and trumpets when they all blow together? Even the slave who tells him the time of day needs to shout in his ear if he is to be heard.'

JUVENAL *Satire* 10.225

Unknowingly, Copa has identified a major reason why the Romans will never become a fully mechanized culture. The Romans have so much cheap manpower available that there is no real incentive to invent machines to do the work or reason to use these machines if they are invented. (Once, someone invented an ingenious crane that would significantly reduce the manpower needed to build the emperor Vespasian's new amphitheatre at the Colosseum. Vespasian rewarded the inventor but declined to use his invention, saying, 'You must allow me to give work to the poor.')

In the same way, some wealthy Romans do not bother with mechanically operated bells and whistles to mark the passing of the hours. It is simpler and cheaper to have a slave boy look at the clock and then run and tell them the time, with the advantage that the same lad can sweep the floor and pour the drinks, too.

⫘ HORA VIII ⫘
(14.00–15.00)

THE BATH ATTENDANT
CHECKS IN CUSTOMERS

*Those baths, where Vulcan pants his flames down the glowing flue
... and the bathers, though exhausted by the intense heat, scorn
the pools and the cold plunge-baths.*

AUSONIUS Mosella 337

In the old days of the Republic, if a Roman wanted to get himself clean he had no choice but to plunge himself into the (sometimes icy) waters of the local *balneum*. This is the often rudimentary bathhouse that still can be found near most of the large apartment blocks in which most inhabitants of Rome live. (The run-off from the baths flushes the latrines in a different part of the same building.) However, in these more decadent days, emperors have discovered that they can buy popularity by expanding these crude stone tubs into huge water parks. These are called *thermae* and they contain not merely washing facilities of all types but other amenities such as gymnasia, libraries and even fast-food franchises. City folk go there not just to get clean but also to socialize and meet business contacts, or to get a workout, massage or shave. It's the perfect way to relax at the end of the working day.

'I came, I saw, I bathed'

The baths are a staple of Roman civilization. Once the legions have settled somewhere for more than a year, one of their first permanent constructions is a bath complex. Often this becomes the nucleus around which a new town forms. Thus we see baths on the frontiers of the empire, such as in Aquincum on the Danube in Pannonia, and at Aquae Sulis in Britain – a town later so well known for this feature that the name will become simply 'Bath'.

While every Roman town has a bath, Rome itself is exceptionally well endowed with them. Given that there are almost 500 baths and almost twice as many temples and shrines, cleanliness is indeed next to godliness for the average Roman. Whether it is a sprawling complex the size of a city block, or a simple set of rooms set into the back of a standard apartment building (these are called *balena*, the main baths are called *thermae*). So there's always a bath nearby, and no excuse for not being clean and sweet-smelling.

The attendant works at the Baths of Nero in the Campus Martius, west of the Forum in the shadow of the mighty dome of Rome's Pantheon. As the poet Martial once ecstatically remarked, 'What could be worse than Nero, or better than his baths?'[10] Indeed, the Neronian baths do reflect the very best of the tyrant emperor's sensual decadence. Red granite and white marble provide the basic colour scheme, and erotic frescoes running (and rolling and writhing) along the walls set the tone. 'Excess in the best possible taste' was Nero's motto, and it has found concrete form in his baths.

BATH HOUSE INTERIOR, POMPEII

On this September day, the bath attendant reckons that there will be between two and five thousand patrons passing through his doors, where they will be greeted by a fountain with a huge bowl over six metres in diameter, the entire thing carved from a single block of red granite. It is still too early for those entering to take the waters. The baths are being flushed and cleaned after their morning's use, and in the basement sweating slaves feed the furnaces that will once again raise temperatures in the *caldarium* to just below blistering. The *caldarium* is the hottest of the baths, and as it takes several days to get the *caldarium* properly heated from a cold start, the fires are seldom allowed to go out completely.

There are four lounging and dressing rooms on each side of the *caldarium*. Here, patrons can get their breath back before bringing their blood back down from boiling point with a plunge into the waters of the self-explanatory *frigidarium*. Those who prefer to avoid extremes can relax in the milder temperatures of the *tepidarium*, which in many baths is not even a pool but simply a modestly heated room. In the Baths of Nero some 1500 square metres of the complex are dedicated to the *caldarium*, *tepidarium* and *frigidarium*, with each area in its own elegant, colonnaded court.

At the baths, he [the emperor Hadrian] gave slaves and money to a veteran soldier whom he knew, because he saw the man rubbing his back and other parts of his body against a marble wall. When asked what he was up to, the soldier replied that he could not afford a slave to massage and scrape him. The next day, there were a number of men rubbing themselves against the wall and trying to attract the attention of the emperor. He called those men to gather in front of him, and told them 'Pair up!'

AELIUS SPARTIANUS *Life of Hadrian* 16

The attendant keeps a wary eye on the *caldarium* court, for in the crowded, bustling baths it is not unusual for light-fingered individuals to quickly rifle through the possessions of the bathers, looking for whatever can be quickly dropped into the fold of a towel and spirited away. For the same reason, though slaves are not allowed to actually use the baths, many bathers bring their slaves with them both to keep an eye on their possessions and to give them a rub and scrape-down afterwards. Romans do not use soap but instead rub scented oil over their bodies and scrape it off afterwards with a curved metal strigil – or a nearby wall if no slave is available. Romans being Romans, even here there's a chance to show off.

We quickly undressed, went into the hot baths and after working up a sweat, passed on to the cold bath. There we found Trimalchio again, his skin glistening all over with perfumed oil. He was not being rubbed down with ordinary linen, but with cloths of the softest, purest wool.

PETRONIUS *The Satyricon*

Apart from keeping slaves from defiling the water, the attendant must be on the lookout for underage bathers. Children are not allowed in the baths, as they risk both drowning and unwanted attention from adults. The 'noisy frequenter of the baths, presenting his armpits to be de-haired and with only an oil flask to conceal his nudity'[11] might well scar a youthful psyche. Because of the nudity issue, bathing facilities often have different times for men and women, with the women usually getting the morning and evening dips. Juvenal gives an example of a noble lady who enjoys bathing late:

She frequents the baths by night; not till dark does she order her oil jars and her household shifted to there. She loves all the bustle of the hot bath; when her arms drop exhausted from using the heavy weights, the anointer passes his hand skilfully over her body, bringing it down at last with a resounding smack upon her thigh.

JUVENAL *Satire* 6

Some bathhouses try to accommodate female clients in the mid-afternoon by having separate facilities built on to the side of the main building. However, these are seldom even close to being as opulent as the main building, and lack many of its facilities. Consequently, ladies of a decadent disposition prefer to delay their pleasure until later in the day, when they can enjoy the sybaritic amenities of the main building.

While they stay open till late, the baths only formally open for men at the eighth hour (2 p.m.), but some early arrivals are already within, using the exercise facilities of the *palestra*, the exercise area under the graceful arches on the eastern wing. Without needing to turn his head, the attendant can hear the rhythmic smacking of a leather ball as players toss it rapidly from hand to hand in a game somewhat resembling volleyball and bruiseball. Then there are the meatier thumps caused by someone taking on a wrestling sack suspended from the ceiling. The basic – and close to the only – rules of Roman wrestling are 'no biting below the belt, or gouging of eyeballs from their sockets', so to avoid unnecessary aggravation, the attendants prefer to match would-be wrestlers with these sacks rather than each other. The attendant is also keeping half an ear on a somewhat overweight individual who is exercising with an ambitiously heavy set of lead weights. The man blows like a winded horse while lifting the weights, and breathes out with a curious whistling sound when he relaxes.

The overall cacophony is bitterly summed up by the philosopher Seneca, who basically had to give up philosophizing in the early afternoon.

I am surrounded by all kinds of noise because my lodgings overlook the baths. Conjure up in your imagination all the sounds that make you hate your own ears.

There're the jocks grunting as they exercise, jerking those heavy weights around. They are working hard – or pretending to. I hear their sharp hissing when they release their pent-up breath. Even if there's a lazy fellow content with a simple massage, you can tell from the slap of hand on shoulder whether it's hitting a flat or a hollow.

If a ballplayer comes up and starts calling out the score, it's game over for me. Add to this the racket of some self-important swine, the thief caught in the act, and the lout who likes the sound of his own voice as he sings in the bath. And, of course, there are those who plunge in the pool with a huge splash of water.

Besides the natural loudmouths, imagine the skinny armpit-hair plucker, whose cries are shrill to draw people's attention. He never stops, except when he's doing his job and making someone else shriek for him. Now add the mingled cries of the drink peddler and the sausage seller, the pastry merchant and other vendors of hot fare, each pushing his products with his own particular yell.

SENECA *Letter* 56.1ff

Like his colleagues, the bath attendant gets a small stipend from the modest entry fee charged to bathers as they arrive (the fee is usually twice as high for women, as the guardians of public morality campaign to keep women at home). However, a lot of the attendant's income comes from tips from performing minor services for the bathers – scraping them down after oiling, looking after their possessions (and, according to scandalous rumour, performing yet more intimate services for female attendees). Therefore, the attendant watches with indignation the antics of sycophants such as Menogenes:

Try every artful trick you can, you can never escape Menogenes at the baths, whether in the hot or cold. When you play ball, he will catch it with eager hands, so that time and again you owe him for having saved a point. When the football lies collapsed he will pick it out of the dirt for you, even though he's in his slippers and has just bathed.

If you bring your own towel, he will pronounce it whiter than snow, though it be dirtier than a baby's bib. As you run the toothed ivory over your balding scalp, he will claim you have coiffured yourself like Achilles. He will bring you the last cupful from the smoky wine jar, and wipe the sweat from your forehead. He praises everything, admires everything, patiently endures sufferings by the thousand until finally you have to ask him 'Will you join me for dinner?'

MARTIAL *Epigrams* 82

Dinner parties are a major component of Roman social life. Who will dine where, with what company and on what foods makes up much of the gossip going around the baths as Rome prepares for the most important meal of the day. Even the bath attendant, as he roams the premises tidying up behind the departing flood of visitors, is making his own dinner plans for the evening.

> *Dasius knows how to count his bathers. He demanded of Spatale, that full-breasted lady, the entrance moneys of three; she gave them.*

> MARTIAL *Epigrams* 51,1

Rome's Top Three Baths (as of AD 123)

1 *The Baths of Trajan*

Sparkling new (completed AD 109) and designed by top architect Apollodorus of Damascus. These baths are set into the Oppian Hill, making them central and highly convenient. They also make good use of a site once occupied by the semi-derelict remains of Nero's once-fabulous Golden House.

There's almost seventy thousand square metres of bathing goodness, divided into pools that hold around eight million litres between them. With frescoes, mosaics and splendid statues, these baths are all you need to refresh body and spirit.

2 *The Baths of Nero*

At twenty-two thousand square metres these baths are tiny in comparison to Trajan's stupendous complex. However, for the thermical aficionado the Baths of Nero have an insidious charm all of their own.

The baths stand near the Baths of Agrippa, which they were evidently meant to outshine (and do), and are supplied by the famously pure, sweet waters of the appropriately named Aqua Virgo. However, there is nothing virginal about the erotic frescoes and embellishments of the inner rooms, which reveal Nero's flamboyant style at its tastefully decadent best.

Those Romans who plan a romantic evening with an *amoratrix* later might first opt for a trip to Nero's to get themselves in the mood.

3 *The Baths of Agrippa*

This was one of the first large bath complexes in the city, built by Augustus' sidekick Agrippa to improve the quality of life in Rome (and, not coincidentally, to improve Augustus' popular support and chances of staying in power). Keeping to a watery theme, the baths are located in the Campus Martius, next to the Basilica of Neptune.

The baths were already showing their age (they were built over a century earlier in 27 BC) before a fire ravaged the bathing complex. As with Agrippa's other signature piece – the Temple of the Pantheon – it will fall to the emperor Hadrian to 'restore' the building to something far more magnificent than the original.

⚏ HORA IX ⚏
(15.00–16.00)

THE HOSTESS ORGANIZES
THE EVENING

The ninth hour commands people to wear out couches piled up with pillows.

MARTIAL *Satires* 4.8.5

It's a man's world in Rome. Take Marcus Aulus Manidus, wealthy, well connected and a big name in the import–export business. He owns over fifty slaves and has a warehouse on the Aventine docks worth tens of thousands of *denarii*. As *paterfamilias* – the head of his family – he has the power of life and death over his two daughters. Should his wife bear him another child, she will place the infant on the ground before him, and should Marcus pick up the child, the babe will be accepted into the family. If he decides not to do so, the baby will be abandoned in the street, to be picked up by any passer-by who wants a child for whatever reason.

Such are the terrible powers vested in the person of Marcus Aulus Manidus. At present, however, the head of the Manidus household is busy taking notes.

'Make sure that awful Fufidus does not push his way to the top couch, as he did last time. I don't know why you invited the fellow. He drones on forever about philosophy, he doesn't bathe often enough, and he's bound to sneer at the gladiators.'

Marcus raises his hand like a schoolboy. 'Um ...' he says, but his wife rolls on.

'Also, remember those are new silk coverlets on the pillows. They cost a fortune, so you make sure – no, you make certain – that no one spills sauce on them. Wool should be good enough, but Aelia has silk cushions in her triclinium, so now I suppose we all have to have them or look as though we are falling behind. Curse the woman! Also ... You, Seluca! Come here!'

The slave woman who had been trying to slink unnoticed past the door comes in warily.

'Any word of the cook? I told you to tell me as soon as he arrives.'

The slave looks harassed.

'No sign of him yet, madam. I'll check again with the doorkeeper, madam.'

'You do that. Marcus! Come back here. We haven't finished yet.'

Marcus sighs and rejoins his spouse. It had not been his idea to have this dinner party anyway. As far as he is concerned, the best way to do business is over several beakers of top-quality wine at his offices near the docks, accompanied by food imported from a local tavern. Then he and his associates can wander around the warehouse, personally inspect the goods, and discuss matters in person with knowledgeable staff. However, Licinia, his companion and helpmeet, has very clear ideas about the social functions 'suitable for a man of his station', and she is determined that he will indulge in those functions, even if it kills him.

ROMAN SIDEBOARD

(And it might. Marcus has a delicate digestion totally unsuited to the rich, oily foods and elaborately spiced sauces that are the staples at Roman dinner parties. He still shudders when he remembers a recent occasion when he carefully avoided the lamprey in garum sauce, the breaded meat and the honey cakes in wine. Despite all this he was nevertheless done in by a beetroot, and spent the next three days camped out in the local latrines.)

Everyone tells Marcus how well he has done to marry Licinia, whose father drops vague references about being related to Rome's aristocratic Licinius clan. Marcus has checked – there's a relationship, sure enough, but nothing to boast about. Several generations back, Licinia's great-great-grandfather was a slave in the household of Licinius Lucullus. When freed, the slave did as all freed slaves do and adopted the *gentilictum* of his manumitter, thus becoming a Licinius. Like many an ambitious freedman with a wealthy and well-connected patron, the newly liberated Licinius had done well for himself – and his descendants.

Licinia doesn't know that Marcus knows what she regards as a shameful family history, and she would be outraged to discover that Marcus doesn't actually care. After all, the poet Horace was the son of a freed slave and he was also the friend and confidant of the emperor Augustus. Even the great Cato the Stoic was descended from a slave woman called Salonia. Slavery is a misfortune that can strike any man – there is certainly no cause to look down on that man's descendants for it. One may as well despise a man for having a weak digestion, though, come to that, Licinia actually does despise this about Marcus.

Knowing why his wife strives so mightily with her social pretensions gives Marcus the endurance to get through the detailed planning that goes into every dinner and soiree of theirs. For this dinner Licinia has decided that their regular cook is not good enough for the occasion, and Marcus must resign himself to eating the fare provided by an outside caterer. The outside chef is highly recommended in Licinia's social circle and this has trumped Marcus' preference for a man he has carefully trained to avoid the foods that give him crippling attacks of indigestion or even more regrettable bouts of flatulence.

' … the signal for the first course to be taken away. I don't want them gorging on the snacks and then not having room for the main course, after all the effort I've put into getting this cook for the occasion. Marcus! Are you even listening?'

The thing is, little as Marcus enjoys such parties, they are an essential part of Roman life. Hosting and attending dinner parties are how Romans of a certain social level get to assess each other's creditworthiness, the quality of their friends and contacts and – a recent preoccupation of Licinia's – the marriageability of their sons. It is also how one gets to hear the latest gossip. This is not just social tittle-tattle but, in an era without newspapers, the way that one hears about a new market opening up in Arabia, or of trading ships wrecked by a storm in the Indian Ocean. These things have a real effect on prices and business decisions, and are well worth risking the malevolent consequences of eating dormice baked in honey.

ROMAN LADY WITH ELABORATE COIFFURE

It's just a pity that Licinia cannot attend the dinner herself – or better still, attend it in Marcus' place. Women can and do attend dinner parties in Rome, but Licinia insists she is not *that* kind of woman, as though a Roman *materfamilias* attending a dinner party were as scandalous as the loose women who attended symposia in the Athens of Pericles. Of course, were she to attend the meal, Licinia would do so sitting properly upright in a chair, rather than sprawled out, three or four to a couch, like the other (male) diners. However, the fact is that most dinners are strictly gender-segregated affairs, and Licinia would no more think of attending one of Marcus' dinners than Marcus would contemplate crashing one of the morning get-togethers that Licinia has with the other wives in her morning salon.

Quintus said as gently as he possibly could, 'Pomponia, could you ask the ladies in [for lunch]; I will invite the men.'

Nothing, I thought, could be put more politely, not only in the actual words, but also in his intentions and his expression. But she, in the hearing of us all, exclaimed, 'Me? I am just a stranger here!'

The origin of that outburst was, I think, the fact that Statius had gone before us to look after the lunch arrangements. [Thus excluding Pomponia from a task that a materfamilias should expect to organize.]

Thereafter, Quintus said to me, 'There, that's what I have to put up with every day.'

You might say, 'Well, what does that amount to?'

Actually, it amounts to a lot. She annoyed even me with the unnecessary vehemence of her reply, not to mention how she looked at him as she gave it. Still, I hid my irritation as we took our places at the table – for which meal she did not appear. Quintus sent the dishes to her room, but she sent them back.

In summary, it seemed to me that no one could have been better-tempered than my brother or more bitchy than your sister.

CICERO TO ATTICUS [POMPONIA'S BROTHER] *Letters* 5.1

Instead, Licinia attends dinner parties by proxy, rigorously coaching Marcus beforehand on what to say, and whom to say it to. Then, while the meal is in progress, Licinia will take time out from making life a misery for the cook in order to interrogate the serving staff on how each course is being received, the general mood of the gathering, and the specific topics being discussed. Licinia also used to have the servants slip little notes to Marcus with in-meal instructions and guidelines until even her mild-mannered spouse was forced to take a stand and point out that it made him appear ridiculous to his fellow diners.

'... make sure it is served only to the people at the top couch. The Mamertine is good enough for the others. Or do you think we should serve those on the bottom couches the last of that Greek wine we got as a gift from one of your clients? If only your other clients were as grateful as ...'

Marcus is vaguely aware that his wife is discussing the dinner wine arrangements. In her opinion – and that of many other Roman hosts – the really good, expensive wine is to be reserved only for those at the top couch in a dinner party. He makes a mental note to quietly but firmly countermand his wife's instructions to the servants and make sure that everyone is served good-quality Massic. Some of those on the lower couches are up-and-coming young men who will remember a slight such as inferior fare, and will repay the insult with interest when they are able.

Cinna, the size of the cups from which I drink, and the size of those from which you drink, are in the proportion of seven to eleven. And yet you complain that you get inferior wine.

MARTIAL *Epigrams* 12.28

A Roman dining room usually has three couches (which is what gives the triclinium its name). Guests recline, propped upon one elbow, three or four on a couch, and take their meal from a table around which the three couches are arranged. Generally, at the end of a course, the servers simply take away the entire table from the open side, and bring in a new one already laden with the dishes for the next course. A dinner party is usually an opportunity for the host to show off his wealth, good taste and powerful connections, so he will try hard to ensure that the food is the best that he – or, rather, his wife – can obtain, and that the food is served to the most influential people he can find.

The other day, I happened to be at dinner with someone whom I do not know particularly well. This fellow (in his own opinion) does things economically but with flair. As far as I can see, he combines the worst of meanness with extravagance.

Elegant dishes were served to me and a favoured few, while everyone else there got cheap fare and scraps. There were also three types of wine in small bottles – not to give the guests a choice, but to remove the power of choice altogether. There was one wine for us and our host, and other sorts for his less and lesser friends (he apparently ranks his friendships by degrees).

PLINY THE YOUNGER *Letters* 19

Among aristocratic Romans it is considered bad form to discuss business or politics while dining. Instead, the talk should be of abstract matters such as poetic criticism, shows of erudition in discussing the origins of rare Latin verbs, and polite yet witty philosophical debate. In the days when she used to send him notes at the table, Licinia would constantly try to get Marcus to steer the conversation in such directions. It never worked, because those at the dinners Marcus attends have never been near an aristocrat's table and have no intention of missing out on the chance to talk shop with their colleagues.

To the distress of Licinia, who is eavesdropping at the door, the talk usually remains resolutely of interest rates, imperial legislation, provincial taxes and grain futures. When it varies from these topics it is usually to discuss the prospects of one or the other teams at the chariot races, or the chances of a renowned gladiator in a forthcoming bout at the arena.

'... before the flute player finishes. Marcus. I do believe you are not listening to a word I say. What is it, girl?'

The 'girl' is the slave woman, Seluca (who, despite the demeaning form of address, is actually a decade older than her mistress). She gulps and then passes on the news that the doorkeeper assures her that the cook has not yet arrived. Their cook is now decidedly late, and since he was bringing his own catering with him, the evening soiree currently has neither food nor anyone to prepare it. Licinia now bitterly regrets giving their own cook the evening off.

There is nothing for it but to send messengers out to the diners asking them to delay their arrival for an hour while every other servant available in the household scours the area around the chef's abode with orders to find the missing cook and bring him to the Manidus household – by force if necessary. Licinia issues her orders with quiet desperation. Marcus might be the host, but the successful planning and execution of a dinner party falls squarely on the shoulders of the *materfamilias* in charge of Marcus' household. If the dinner party is anywhere near the failure it currently threatens to be, Licinia can expect to endure the cooing mock-sympathy of her peers for weeks to come.

She glares at her husband. 'This is all your fault ...'

[Romans took their own napkins to a dinner party. They did not always return with them.]

Hermogenes, it seems to me, is as great a thief
of napkins, as Massa was of money.
Even though you watch his right hand, and hold his left,
he will find a way to filch your napkin.
...
When at last, knowing it would be stolen,
nobody brought a napkin with him,
Hermogenes stole the cloth from the table.
...
However dreadfully hot it gets in the theatre,
They whip the awnings away when Hermogenes turns up.
The sailors, in trembling haste, proceed to furl up their sails
Should Hermogenes show himself in the harbour.
...
Hermogenes has never taken a napkin to dinner;
Hermogenes has never left a dinner without one.

MARTIAL *Epigrams* 12.29

☷ HORA X ☷

(16.00–17.00)

THE WASHERWOMAN
DOES A LATE SHIFT

'I sing of fullers and the owl, not of arms and the man'

Graffiti from the *Fullonica of Fabius Ululitremulus*
(Pompeii *Corpus Inscriptiones Latinarum* 4.9131)[12]

Anyone looking for Caecilius the cook – as the slaves of the Manidus household are currently doing – will do as the slaves of the Manidus household and leave the yard of Thais the Fuller as the very last place to check. This is not because Caecilius is not there often – in fact, because he and Thais are romantically involved, the cook spends a lot of time there. However, the aromas of the yard are so overpowering that the slaves prefer to spend more time looking in better-smelling places where Caecilius probably isn't, than in the odoriferous hall where he probably is.

The sad fact is that, apart from tanners' yards, not many places in Rome stink worse than a laundry. And tanners' yards are relegated by law to the Transtiberim district west of the Tiber. However, since laundry work is a specialized job and no Roman washes his own clothes, there is a laundry catering to the general public on almost every second residential block in the city – so there's really no escaping the smell.

The *fullonica* of Thais is typical of such establishments. It is a large, airy building designed to catch every passing breeze and waft it through the hall's interior. Thais, like every fuller, is preoccupied with getting fresh air to her workers for the simple reason that they are quite likely to die if they don't get it. The chemicals used in cleaning the clothes here are that potent – and pungent. The slave approaching this building in his search for Caecilius knows what he is getting close to because of the combination of two smells that assault his nostrils as he gets to the door – sulphur and stale urine.

Men's urine relieves gout, as is shown by the testimony of fullers, who for that reason claim that they never suffer from this malady.

PLINY *Natural History* 28.18

The Romans believe that washing clothes in urine makes whites whiter and colours brighter, and this magic ingredient also removes stubborn stains. And the Romans are right. Yes, that wonder material, human pee, is what every *materfamilias* relies on for her husband's shining white toga and her seductively dyed filmy nightwear. This is because urine contains the special component ammonia, which will still feature in washing powders two millennia hence. In a pre-chemical era, the best way to get ammonia is from those cheap and self-powered dispensaries known as human bladders.

What urine actually contains is urea and lots of nitrogen. The fuller mixes this with a touch of earth and leaves it in an open jug for a week. The bacteria in the earth get to work chomping through the nitrogen in the urine (this nitrogen content is also why urine can be used as a fertilizer) and produce ammonia as a by-product. Another by-product of the process is a choking miasma that fills the room and induces instant nausea in the inexperienced.

Ammonia is needed for washing clothing because human skin is rich in glands that produce an oily, waxy substance called sebum. This protects and moistens the skin, and on a hot summer's day in Rome its chemicals emulsify the sweat of Romans so that it becomes a cooling sheen on the skin rather than rolling off in drops. The problem with sebum is that it rubs off on to clothing, making garments greasy and later grimy, as the grease attracts dirt. Normal water won't do a thing to shift that dirt. Water, with added 'Special P' as an extra ingredient, uses ammonia to break down the grease and so produces cleaner clothes.

But wait! There's more! Roman clothing is coloured by dyes, which are made from natural materials such as seeds, leaves, lichens, bark and berries. These are not fixed dyes. They not only come out in the wash but will do so even during normal use, unless they are fixed to the cloth fibres by a chemical agent known as a 'mordant'. This binds to the chromophores that give a dye its colour, and surrounds it with a protective web. The best mordants in a pre-industrial society are found in – you guessed it – stale urine.

When the slave looking for the cook comes across Thais, she is supervising the stacking of the day's urine harvest. This is in the form of large urns, which Thais has strategically placed expressly for that purpose at street corners, recesses in alleyways and the back rooms of select taverns. Romans don't have to spend a penny when relieving themselves, because the act is subsidized by Thais: ever since the mid-first century, fullers have had to pay a tax for every urn they use to collect nature's bounty.

When his son Titus objected because Vespasian had put a tax on fullers' urns, Vespasian held a coin from the first payment to his son's nose. 'Does it smell?'

SUETONIUS *Life of Vespasian* 23[13]

While the urns are being stacked, other slaves are draining the soaking pools in the hall's courtyard. As mentioned earlier, Roman dyes are not colour-fast, so one pool is needed for pale greens, another for deep greens, another for browns, and so on. The pools contain a mixture of water, diluted dye and warm urine, and they are regularly drained to prevent them from becoming too foetid. During the working day, clothes that are deposited by the client will be left here to soak. (Thais keeps a careful record of who has deposited what, because if there is a mix-up or clothes get lost or damaged, they have to be replaced or repaired at her expense.)

There are three ways of telling people who work at a fuller's. One is the acrid smell that seems to permeate from the fuller's very pores, and another is that they tend to cough a lot, because however well aired a *fullonica*, the mix of pungent detergents eventually corrodes the lungs. Finally, the slaves all have legs like champion

Olympians. This is because once the clothes have had a good soak, they are transported to the now-vacant stalls lining two sides of the halls and placed in tubs. During the day, the slaves stand in the stalls and leap up and down on the clothes to pound the ammonia into the fibres. This leap is called the 'fuller's stomp' and is practised in gymnasia by those wanting to develop their leg muscles. Those who have no choice but to do it all day, every day, end up with very well-developed legs.

Thais turns a questioning look at the newcomer, but this is wasted. Firstly, because the hall is already too gloomy for her expression to be determined, and secondly, because the visitor is in the middle of a sneezing fit from a small cloud of sulphur that a stray breeze has wafted down the hall. It's mainly togas that get the sulphur treatment, because the volatile elements in the steam from burning sulphur are good at breaking down stains.

←──→

But she's been hiding her passion for a secret lover. He meets her constantly to share stolen embraces. In fact, she and her young man were energetically making love when we [her husband and I] returned early from the baths for dinner.

Our distressingly sudden arrival forced the wife to act quickly. So she shoved her lover into the sulphur cage. This was a funnel of smooth wicker sticks with a narrow opening at the top. (They hang clothes on it to bleach in the fumes from the smouldering sulphur.)

With her lover safely stashed away she happily joined her husband at the table. However, the lad was having a tough time amid the choking fumes and the acrid penetrating smoke. Finally,

the dense mass of fumes started to suffocate him, while the active
elements of the sulphur did as they usually do, and caused him to
sneeze – and go on sneezing.

APULEIUS *The Golden Ass* 9.22ff

Irritably, Thais yells down the hall for the slaves to 'move the tent'. The slaves do this readily enough, for the request is far from uncommon and the atmosphere in the hall is choking enough already. When a toga is removed from the stomping bowl, it is usually wrung out and hung to dry. (The effort of wringing out the forty to sixty soaking wet square feet of wool that make up the average toga ensures that the forearms of the establishment's staff are just as muscular as their legs.) A toga is semi-circular in shape when it is not draped elegantly around its Roman wearer, and this makes it easy to drape over the curved frame of flexible wands used for drying and smoking a toga.

While one 'toga tent' is smoking over the sulphur fumes, the slaves work on another, currying it with hedgehog skin to raise the nap (the threads on the surface of the fabric) – a process that both makes the fabric of the toga look thicker and more luxuriant and also ensures that the sulphur gets into every nook and cranny. If the toga is for a particularly special occasion, the fuller might have been asked to prepare a *toga candida*. These togas are extra-white because they have been scrubbed with Cimolus earth, which adds a particular pearly lustre to the garment.

Fullonica of Stephanus (on the Decumanus Maximus)

*Fullonica
A laundry cum dyer cum presser (a toga press was found in situ)*

ROMAN LAUNDRY (FULLONICA) IN POMPEII

Politicians have paid particular attention to the *toga candida* because this is worn by anyone standing for public office (which is why those so standing are called 'candidates'). The legislation is very precise, and has been recorded by the naturalist Pliny the Elder:

> *A law referring to fullers still stands ... The prescribed process is as follows: the cloth is first washed with Sarda earth [from Sardinia], and then it is steamed with sulphur. Assuming that the dye is good, the garment should afterwards by scoured with Cimolus earth; if it*

is coloured with bad dye, this becomes obvious as it turns black and
the sulphur makes the colours run. However, Cimolian earth adds
depth and lustre to properly treated garments.

PLINY *Natural History* 35.57

Between his coughs and sneezes, the slave manages to choke out his query about the whereabouts of the missing cook. Thais glares at the man, uncertain of whether he is making fun of her and her establishment by over-dramatizing the atmosphere. Thais herself has been hanging around laundries since she was a little girl, for she inherited the business from her father. She genuinely cannot smell the stench everyone goes on about.

This is what later ages will call 'odour habituation'. Just as those living next door to a blacksmith eventually become so accustomed to the clang of hammer on metal that they cease to register it, so Thais' brain has long ago learned to disregard the scent of ammonia-packed urine as simply not relevant to her daily activities. She sometimes has to check if a jug is ready for use by leaning over it to smell the bouquet, despite the fact that the smell can knock a visitor flat at twenty paces.

⟵―――――――――――――――――――――――――――⟶

Thais smells worse than a greedy fuller's urn
that's just broken in the middle of the street ...
worse than a jar foetid with spoilt pickle.
Cunningly wishing to overlay this odour with another
She discards her clothes and enters the bath
Green with depilatory, and half-hidden
Under a layer of chalk dissolved in acid ...

Then she thinks she's made herself safe.
Yet despite a thousand artifices, in the end
Thais still smells of Thais.

MARTIAL *Epigrams* 6.93

←——————————————————————————————→

This can occasionally be a problem – for example, when she pulls on an improperly rinsed *stola* and finds herself walking the crowded streets of Rome with a six-foot bubble of clear space on the pavement around her. It certainly plays hell with her love life. Usually, a woman like Thais would have no problem attracting males, for her Asiatic Greek ancestry has given her lustrous, curly dark hair, large, expressive brown eyes with a slightly exotic slant, and an hourglass figure well muscled by the exigencies of her job.

Caecilius the cook, on the other hand, is no great catch, for though the man is a wonder with a skillet and catfish, he is physically somewhat puny with a receding chin and pale, watery eyes. However, cookery has habituated him to powerful smells, and he does like a woman with an appetite. Watching Thais plough through a trencher of mussels and spelt is a heart-warming experience for a man who sometimes feels that his efforts are unappreciated.

But Caecilius is not here right now, and Thais brusquely informs the slave to that effect. He had to cancel their evening plans because he had drawn a cooking gig with some merchant family on the Caelian Hill. Sorry.

The slave is about to mention that it is precisely because Caecilius is *not* at his 'cooking gig' that he is here. However, at that moment one of the workers sloshes an amphora full of well-matured *eau de Romana naturel* into the soaking pool behind him. The mixture also contains crushed and soaked fennel and onion skins to enhance the colour of the orange fabrics that will be washed therein. A wave of liquorice odour from the fennel combined with the smell of rotten onions in ammonia turns the slave a pale shade of green. He gurgles his thanks and flees from the premises, leaving a bemused Thais staring at his back.

∏ HORA XI ∏
(17.00–18.00)

THE COOK GETS FRANTIC

I would prefer the dishes on my table to please the diners rather than the cook.

MARTIAL *Epigrams* 9.81

As he toils up the hill laden with his special ingredients and specialized cooking implements, Septimius Caecilius is seen by a household slave, who rushes from the portals of the Manidus home to urgently inform the chef that he is late. As if Caecilius did not know.

He snarls in reply, 'I thank you for the information. If I later stick your head into my oven, do please inform me that it is hot.'

The cook has not had a good afternoon. Ever since meeting the hostess Licinia five days ago and discussing arrangements for the dinner, Caecilius has been aware that this is one meal that will be cooked as a team effort. That is, the hostess will watch over his shoulder and supply a constant stream of comments, suggestions and criticisms about the preparation of the food, all of which Caecilius will ignore.

It's not as if he does not know how to cook *tetrapharmacum*. Ever since the dish has been popularized by the emperor, it has necessarily become a part of every chef's repertoire. And that's the problem. Of course, the meal is diabolically complex to prepare. After all, if it were easy, then specialized cooks like Caecilius could not make a living. The meal is made up of 'four drugs' (which is what *tetrapharmacum* actually means). These 'drugs' are pheasant, wild boar, ham in pastry, and sow's udders. (There used to be an added ingredient of peacock, but – frankly – that's just for show. Pheasant is easier to get and tastes much better.)

What kind of feasts did the emperor indulge in when something costing so much money was just a side dish of a modest dinner party? Something to be burped up by a purple-clad parasite …

JUVENAL *Satire* 4

The pheasant is easily procured at the market, which Caecilius visited that morning. The ham in pastry is even easier, as getting the ham simply involved lifting it off the shelf in his own larder. The pastry dough, light and flaky, is wrapped in a thin leather sachet, waiting to be rolled out in the Manidus kitchen. Wild boar sounds as though it might be tricky to obtain, but Caecilius has connections with the butchers, who alert him whenever a fresh supply comes in. Also, wild boar is meant to taste a touch gamey, so the fact that his meat has – ahem – matured is not really an issue. The problem is the sow's udders.

BUYING HARES AT A MARKET STALL

All the other ingredients are packed into the udder and come tumbling out when it is slit. Therefore, you need a large udder. Which means you need a sow that is suckling piglets. Which means you need a peasant who is prepared to sacrifice a breeding sow before his piglets are weaned. And you have to beat every other chef in Rome to those udders, because word of udders for sale does for chefs what blood in the water does for sharks.

Consequently, Caecilius had tried his very best to steer the hostess towards other dishes. He cunningly hinted of the exotic charms of tiger steak or fillet of giraffe. (A show staged at the Colosseum recently saw the death of these and other animals by the hundred. The Romans have a 'waste not, want not' attitude to such things, and almost every creature slaughtered in the arena eventually finds its way on to a Roman dinner table. Caecilius has even tried crocodile, which he found unexpectedly tender and juicy, rather like prime chicken.)

While the hostess's interest was piqued, Licinia had decided that, with her reputation at stake, she would rather play safe. A high-society lady might be able to laugh it off if her minced elephant was in poor taste, but someone struggling up the social ladder cannot take that chance.

In that case, suggested Caecilius, the hostess might like to try his speciality signature dish. There was never a dinner party but that was ecstatic about it. Who doesn't like milk-fed snails fried in olive oil with a putrefied fish gut dressing? Caecilius has a special cage in his own kitchen with a collection of *Helica pomatia*, the Roman edible snail. When an order for dinner comes in, the snails are dunked in jars containing a mix of milk, vine must and barley flour. Every few hours, a slave clears away the excrement as the snails gorge themselves until they are too fat to get back into their shells. Then they are ready for frying in the most delicate of first-press extra-virgin olive oils.

To top off this gustatory extravaganza, Caecilius measures out two teaspoons of *liquamen*. This salty fish sauce is highly prized by the Romans, who import thousands of *amphorae* of the stuff from Spain every year. *Liquamen* is best prepared out in the hot Spanish sun, where fish intestines are thrown into salted water and left to liquefy. The result is strained through a fine cloth so that the liquid (rich in proteins and vitamin B) is sold as *liquamen*, and the semi-solid remainder as *garum* sauce.

A Recipe for Lentils with Coriander

Boil the lentils. Once the mix foams [scoop off the scum] and add [chopped] leeks and green coriander. If it's not already crushed, crush the coriander seed with pennyroyal, laser root and seeds of mint and rue. Moisten the mix with honey and vinegar, some garum [use soy sauce if garum is unavailable] and defrutum [grape syrup if your local market does not stock defrutum]. Finally add olive oil and sprinkle with pepper when the lentils are almost done.

Apicius 192

Caecilius had waxed positively poetic in describing this culinary delight, but to no avail. Licinia was adamant. If *tetrapharmacum* is good enough for the emperor's table, then it can certainly grace hers. The starter – thrushes baked into small bread loaves – and the dessert – honey-cakes in wine – can be selected and prepared at the chef's discretion. But if he is not going to cook *tetrapharmacum* for her, Licinia will find a chef who will.

In desperation, Caecilius sent one of his servants to do the rounds of smallholdings outside Rome, ordering the man to buy the whole pig if necessary, as long as he came back with the prized udders. Over the morning, as he got the other ingredients ready, Caecilius waited with ever-increasing anxiety for the servant to return. When he did – to Caecilius' murderous despair – the man was empty-handed.

A Recipe for Meatless Sausages

Pour must [yeasty wine in the early stage of fermentation] over flour and add [crushed] anise and cumin seeds. Mix in lard [or vegetable shortening] and grated cheese [goat's cheese works well]. Knead the mixture into dough, and form rolls. Put a bay leaf under each. Bake until ready.

CATO *De Agricultura* 121

There was nothing for it but for Caecilius to take the chef's action of last resort and throw himself at the mercy of his peers. The servant was sent around other kitchens of the city, enquiring if anyone had sow's udders available, and letting it be known that Caecilius was prepared to offer everything including his first-born son in return. It was late afternoon before the servant scored a hit. A chef by the Tiber Island had been preparing *tetrapharmacum* for a dinner party that a priestess of Isis was giving for local grandees.

At the last moment, the priestess had discovered that, on account of several of the local grandees being Jewish, sow's udders were firmly off the menu. If Caecilius was able to supply a set of his famous jugged hare as a replacement, the chef said, he could have the udders. This necessitated Caecilius going to the Tiber Island in person and at a sprint, carrying with him several fillets of fresh(ish) Pontic sturgeon. The priestess' cook was startled to discover that the jugged hare would have violated Jewish dietary requirements as comprehensively as pork, and the chef gratefully surrendered the sow's udders in exchange for the fish.

As a bonus, the udders have already been cleaned, marinated and prepared, so that all Caecilius has to do when he gets to the Manidus household is stuff them with his readied ingredients and get baking. Caecilius has sent a servant ahead to prepare the oven at the dinner-party premises and get started on the thrushes. So he is alone when he sets off, late and already exhausted. With his servant gone, he has to carry all his gear himself, loaded down like the proverbial donkey.

The reminder of his lateness from the slave who met Caecilius outside the house is the mildest of rebukes compared to the outpouring of invective with which Licinia greets her errant cook. Caecilius cuts her off brusquely yet politely.

'Mistress, we can discuss my difficulties in getting here, or I can prepare dinner for your guests. If you choose the former, I stand here at your disposal.'

Caecilius is very glad he is not the slave chef at a wealthy household, where such impudence would result – at the very least – in a sound whipping. It's not unusual for such cooks to be physically chastised even in the course of a meal, and the poet Martial mentions hosts who would 'sooner cut open the cook than his rabbit'. The worst that Caecilius can lose is his reputation, and since Licinia's reputation is at stake as well, he knows that she will back down from his ultimatum.

← ─── →

A tray supporting an enormous hog was set on the table. One and all we expressed our admiration at the speed at which it had been cooked, and swore that a mere ordinary fowl could not have been roasted in that time. This was all the more impressive as the hog appeared to be a much larger animal than the wild boar of the previous course. After a few seconds Trimalchio, who had been staring harder and harder at the meal, exclaimed, 'No! No! Has it been gutted? No! by the Gods – it hasn't. Summon the cook!'

The cook came in. He stood by the table. Chagrined, he sadly admitted that it had completely slipped his mind – he had clean forgotten. 'Slipped his mind?' yelled Trimalchio. 'Listen to him! You would think he had forgotten to add a pinch of pepper or a touch of cumin. Strip him [for a whipping]!'

Moments later, the cook was stripped. He looked abjectly miserable between two of Trimalchio's henchmen. Everyone started to intervene on the cook's behalf, saying, 'These things happen. Forgive him this once and if he ever does it again, not a soul will speak up for him.'

Personally, I was unrelenting in my outrage. I could not stop myself from leaning over and muttering in [my friend] Agamemnon's ear, 'He has to be a diabolically bad servant. By Jupiter, how do you forget to gut and clean a hog? If it were up to me, the man could expect no mercy even if he'd been so careless with a fish.'

But Trimalchio was grinning all over his face. 'All right, then!' proclaimed he. 'If your memory is so bad, do the disembowelling now so we can all see that you have done it.'

So ordered, the cook tremulously took up his knife and slashed it across the animal's belly. The cut widened under the pressure from within and out tumbled a feast of sausages and black puddings.

At this all the servants applauded as one ... and the cook was rewarded with a beaker of wine.

PETRONIUS *Satyricon* 49–50

The kitchen is baking hot, as it should be. Caecilius offers his thanks to his servant and to Fornax, the goddess of ovens, that all is ready to go as soon as he has unpacked his ingredients. The house is equipped with the standard Roman oven, which is a low structure built against the wall. This is usually brick or tile, with room for two semi-circular fireplaces and a large, flat clay top.

A variety of pots stand on the shelf beside the ovens, and Caecilius regards these with an expert eye. The oven itself is basically two open fires in arched fireplaces in which the logs have burned down to large coals. To bake in this oven, one selects a pot of the appropriate size and thickness, adds basting and whatever other ingredients are required and inserts the entire pot into the oven. Then it is a matter of careful timing to make sure the clay of the pot stays at the right temperature by moving it about, or even out of the coals, and all the while stirring the sauces in copper pans heated on the oven's flat top. Remove the pot, gingerly untwine the wire holding closed the lid – and presto! One well-baked meal, ready for the table.

Good quality the oven might be, but the rest of the room is unimpressive. Like many kitchens, even at top-class Roman homes, this one is a rather pokey affair into which the master of the household seldom ventures. The mistress is another story, though, as she regards it as part of her duties to ensure that the cook is not siphoning off household money through extravagant purchases, or pretending to pay top *denarius* for ingredients while getting sub-standard goods and pocketing the difference. Caecilius is pleased to see that this kitchen is sensibly stocked, at least, and the regular cook, as requested, has laid out all the herbs and cooking utensils he will need. Perhaps the meal will go smoothly after all.

As Licinia sarcastically suggests that Caecilius might like to get started on the actual cooking, the doorman pops his head around the kitchen door. One of the workers from the *fullonica* of Thais has turned up, sent by Caecilius' girlfriend to search him out and inform him that he is wanted by someone. Apparently he's late preparing their dinner.

⫿ HORA XII ⫿
(18.00–19.00)

THE PRIESTESS PREPARES
TO SACRIFICE

Una quai es omnia, Dea Iset – Being one, you are everything,
Goddess Isis

INSCRIPTION OF A ROMAN CHANT TO THE GODDESS

The priestess sighs and looks at the sturgeon steaks left by the cook Caecilius. These men are meant to be professional chefs. So why, in the name of the Goddess, can't they be bothered to find out the dietary needs of their customers? First, that ignoramus of a cook she had hired was preparing sow's udders. This despite knowing that she has several Jewish guests coming to her late dinner. Surely, the one thing everyone in Rome knows about Jews is that they do not eat pork?

Actually, the priestess herself does not eat swine flesh either. It amazes her that many of her fellow Romans do, since the pig is so unclean an animal. Furthermore, of all the beasts, the pig is most inclined to mate under a waning moon, when the forces of life are ebbing. What good can come from a creature conceived in this manner?

On top of all this, as the priestess patiently explained to her cook (while refraining from an unpriestly urge to belt him over the head), it is well known to the Egyptians that those who drink of the milk of pigs break out in leprosy and scabrous itching. Yet he wants to feed her guests the very udders in which that milk is created? What dessert was he planning – essence of deadly nightshade served on wolfsbane cakes?

Then enter that supercilious Caecilius, so proud of himself for knowing that Jewish people do not eat the flesh of the hare either – something else her profoundly ignorant cook had not known. Yet he had brought fish – as if a priestess of Isis can eat fish! Certainly, other Egyptians eat fish, and indeed religious reasons dictate that they must broil their fish on the ninth day of the first month. The priestess buys the fish, since her religion dictates that on that day she must. But she lets the fish keep right on cooking in its little stove on the pavement outside her house, until it burns up in front of her door.

The fish is an impure creature, for it comes from the sea, and the sea is a superfluous element, unwanted material left over from the creation. The sea is useless for ploughing or drinking or any other purpose whatsoever, and if the gods did not see fit to make use of the sea, their priestess will certainly not consume the fruits of its unholy, impure and tainted waters. Indeed, the priestess would like to drink only from the waters from which the ibis, the sacred bird, has sipped, just as the priests at the great temple at Philae in holy Egypt do – for, as they say, the pure should never touch the impure – and the ibis will only drink of unpolluted water.

Blessed Queen of the heavens, sweet mother of mankind, who with your grace and bounty nourish all, even the most wretched of the world. No day, night or a single instant passes without your blessings. You protect mankind on land and sea, mitigate the tempests of misfortune and stay [malign] destinies written in the stars. The gods above adore you, and the gods below give you honour.

...

At your command the winds blow, the clouds water the land, seedlings sprout and bring forth fruit. The birds above, the beasts of the mountains, the serpents in their lairs, even the monsters of the deep tremble at your power.

My spirit is too poor to sing your full praises, my wealth of words too petty to offer as sacrifice. I have not the words to offer what is in my heart. Nor would I yet have enough with a thousand tongues in a thousand mouths. All your poor worshipper can do is remember you always and hold the vision of you within my heart.

APULEIUS *The Golden Ass* 11.25ff

Purity is important to followers of the goddess Iset, whom the Romans call Isis. For this reason, as she prepares to sacrifice, the priestess dons a robe of linen. Unlike wool, which grows from flesh that ages, corrupts and dies, the flax from which linen is derived comes from the eternal and undying earth. The priestess, in preparation for the sacrifice, has removed every hair from her body as superfluous and impure. Why then would she thereafter clothe herself in the hair of animals? Linen is plain, clean and is less likely to harbour lice.

Furthermore, her robe was harvested when the flax was in bloom, and even undyed, the linen shimmers with the azure blue of the sky. Why swap such a garment for a scratchy robe of wool? Now, the priestess contemplates the meal she will be hosting after the sacrifice. Basically, it's about community relations. Every nation under the sun has a complement of its peoples in Rome. There are Britons, red-faced and peeling, unaccustomed to the Italian heat; there are swarthy Moors from the deep deserts of Africa; and once she even met a man who claimed to be from fabled China, the land of dragons, silk and legends.

Unlike Jewish followers of their One God, and the Palestinian worshippers of Ba'al in his many forms, the followers of Isis are a cosmopolitan lot. Iset, the Egyptian mother-god, is now Isis the Compassionate, to whom Greeks, Romans, Celtiberians, Isaurians and many others pray. Of course, they also pray to other gods, and all (except the Jews and Christians, whom the priestess regards as frankly insane) pray to the emperor and great Jupiter, guardian of Rome. Even the priestess herself is a henotheist, which means that, though dedicated to Isis, she acknowledges the existence of other gods, and will even pray to them on occasion.

PRIESTESS STATUE FROM THE ISAEUM IN POMPEII

All About Isis

We know much more about the religion of Isis than other contemporary religions, because the contemporary writer (and priest) Plutarch was fascinated by – and rather respectful of – the goddess. His text *On Isis and Osiris* is packed full of details of Isean beliefs and rituals.

One issue affecting the priestess is that there is a large Jewish population in her district. (Jews like to live together, as that way schools, synagogues and butchers catering to their requirements are all at hand.) However, due to their strict monotheism, the Jews do not join in the major celebrations of her religion – which being fun, colourful and providing lavish amounts of free food, are enthusiastically enjoyed by most Romans. The 5 March celebration had been a procession from the major temple of Isis, the Iseum Campense on the Campus Martius, to the river near the Tiber Island. There, a boat had been formally blessed as representative of the boat in which Isis travelled the world looking for body parts of her beloved Horus, scattered across the earth by the evil god Set.

As well as being full of life and colour, the festivals are noisy, rowdy affairs. The bearded elders whom the priestess will be entertaining tonight wish to be reassured that the late October festival will be quieter, more restrained and less distressing to their congregation. At this October festival – well, to be honest, at this street party with religious overtones – the role of Isis in the death and resurrection of the god Serapis will be enthusiastically celebrated. The task of the priestess tonight – helped, she hopes, by fillets of well-prepared sturgeon – will be to tell the elders diplomatically that no, the party will be noisy, unrestrained and riotous as ever, and they might as well get used to the idea.

After all, the followers of Isis mostly conduct their affairs out of the public eye, in temples and shrines closed off from the masses. Unlike the ceremonies dedicated to the gods of Rome, which are very public affairs, many of the rites to Isis are mysteries from which the profane are excluded. Even the sacrifice that the priestess is to perform tonight will be done within the closed walls of the shrine, with only two acolytes in attendance. So, twice a year the festivals of Isis break out into the public domain. These festivals are also recruiting drives as the curious ask devotees about the goddess and her rites. The rest of the year, the shrine of Isis and the local synagogues and churches get along amicably, apart from the odd – sometimes very odd – Christian preacher standing outside the shrine and denouncing it as a den of wickedness and harlotry. (A misplaced charge. Though prostitutes often hang around Roman temples where the portico keeps them out of the rain and the wind, followers of Isis are actually less profligate than members of the general public. This is because their religion requires periods of sexual abstinence before certain religious celebrations.)

And so we came to the day of the sacrifice. At nightfall, many priests arrived … and all the laity profane were ordered off the premises. They put a linen robe on my back and then conducted me to the innermost and most secret and sacred part of the temple.

Now, being a dedicated student, you may wish to know what was said and done while I was there. And indeed I would tell you, if it were lawful for me to tell. But if it was proper for you to know, you would know already. Should I further indulge your rash curiosity, both your ears and my tongue would suffer for it.

APULEIUS *The Golden Ass* 11.23

The time is passed when the Roman authorities used to persecute the followers of Isis, and the priestess intends to gently remind her guests of this fact. She also plans to mention that it was precisely because followers practised their religion quietly and in private that the suspicion of the senate of the Roman Republic was aroused. Although to tell the truth, the senate also did not like the cosmopolitan nature of the congregation. Slaves, foreigners and the dispossessed rubbed shoulders with well-born ladies and the occasional aristocrat during ceremonies, making the cult temples of the goddess ideal places for revolutions to foment.

The result was that in 50 BC, private temples to Isis were banned, and the consul personally led a gang of priests and workmen to physically de-consecrate one such temple. The workmen staged an impromptu strike, pointing out that this was a temple to a great goddess and knocking the place down might attract her unfavourable attention. Thereupon, the consul – one Aemilius Paullus – had shrugged off his toga, picked up an axe and started work on the temple doors in person. Anti-Isis sentiments reached a peak in the time of Augustus, when all temples of Isis were forcibly removed from within the *pomerium*, Rome's sacred boundary (this is the reason why the priestesses' shrine is near the Tiber Island, just outside that boundary). However, Augustus had finished the civil wars by campaigning against Mark Antony and his close ally Cleopatra of Egypt. In her propaganda, Cleopatra had claimed to be Isis reincarnate. What the goddess had thought of that particular idea can easily be deduced from what happened to Cleopatra and Mark Antony thereafter. The goddess does not like those who adopt her name in vain.

The emperor Tiberius had even those shrines torn down, and statues of the goddess thrown into the river. However, both Caligula and Nero (emperors not averse to a good time) had been supporters of Isis. The emperor Domitian certainly had been, because when his father Vespasian declared war on the then government of Rome,

Domitian fled Rome to safety in the guise of a cultist of Isis. Also – as the priestess won't remind her guests unless it comes to an out-and-out napkin-flinging beard-pulling fight – before formally celebrating their triumph over the Jews in the war of AD 64–70 the emperor Vespasian and his son Titus had previously spent the required night of purification in a temple of Isis.

Isidore

Just as the name 'Theodore' means 'Gift of God' so the name 'Isidore' means 'Gift of Isis'. This gives us something of a glimpse into the respective religions of the parents of what turned out to be the rather confusingly named church father St Isidore of Seville. Thereafter, two patriarchs of the medieval Greek Orthodox Church (Isidore I and Isidore II) also proclaimed themselves to be gifts of the goddess.

Given this level of imperial support, the chances of the delegation getting the authorities to force the cult to tone down its celebrations are officially zero. The current emperor Hadrian is rather keen on Egypt and things Egyptian, as was Hadrian's predecessor, Trajan. These days, the worship of Isis is thoroughly respectable. If things do get rather loose twice a year, well, it's still pretty respectable compared to, for example, those goings-on at the officially sanctioned Floralia Celebrations in late April, which features licentiousness in dozens of ingenious varieties.

Having rehearsed her arguments, the priestess prepares to cross the street between her house and the shrine. From behind the walls of the shrine – unlike 'official' Roman temples, shrines and temples to Isis are closed off from the street – comes the bleating of the kid that will be tonight's sacrifice. The priestess is rather pleased with the animal, which has red hair and is therefore abhorrent to the gods. The Romans believe that the gods prefer the sacrifice of animals most pleasing to them – for example, Janus likes a Ram, and Mars, God of War, demands a horse every October. Yet the commonsensical religion of Isis can see the flaw in this reasoning. If you sacrifice an animal pleasing to the gods, well, you kill it. Surely, the creatures the gods would prefer to see killed are those they dislike and would rather see taken off the face of the earth. (There's a complex theological reason why the Egyptian gods don't like red-haired animals, which we need not go into here.)

Originally, the priestess would throw the head of the sacrificed animal into the Tiber. However, after watching her do this a few times, the Asiatic butcher down the road made a good offer for the heads of sacrificial beasts. After consultation with the temple, the priestess discovered that this more profitable form of disposal was also ecumenically correct, so she expects to spend a while tomorrow morning haggling over her victim's remains.

Tonight, before she begins the sacred mysteries of the sacrifice, there is the more mundane matter of finding out what the cook has prepared for her in place of the forbidden sturgeon. Rather sulkily, the chef admits that he has decided to play completely safe and eschew meat altogether. He informs the priestess that she will be having a simple yet elegant dinner of barley cakes with chopped onion and nuts. The priestess looks at the cook blankly.

'Onions? I can't eat onions!'

Nothing that is irrational or fabulous or prompted by superstition, as some believe, has ever been given a place in their [Isean] rites, but in them are some things that have moral and practical values, and others that are not without their share in the refinements of history or natural science, as, for example, that which has to do with the onion.

For the tale that Dictys, the nurseling of Isis, in reaching for a clump of onions fell into the river and was drowned is extremely incredible. But the priests keep themselves clear of the onion and detest it and are careful to avoid it, because it is the only plant that naturally thrives and flourishes in the waning of the moon.

It is suitable for neither fasting nor festival, because in the one case it causes thirst and in the other tears for those who partake of it.

PLUTARCH *On Isis and Osiris 8*
(trans Plut. Mor. Vol.V of Loeb Classical Library, 1936)

▥ HORA NOCTIS I ▥
(19.00–20.00)

THE SPICE TRADER SETS
OUT FOR DINNER

Nowadays, voyages are made to India every year, with a troop
of archers carried on board the merchantmen, as those seas are
swarming with pirates.

PLINY *Natural History* 6.26

As her husband sets off, the wife of Miyrius the spice trader kisses
him on the cheek and tells him, 'Come safely home again.' She says
the same thing whether he is setting out on a two-year voyage to
Alexandria and their native Syria, or if he is doing as he is tonight
and going out to dinner for a few hours. Not that dinner with
Marcus Manidus is without its perils, Miyrius notes with a gentle
shudder. When a messenger arrived to tell him that dinner would

be delayed, Miyrius did speculate for a moment on whether this was because the hostess, Licinia, had eaten the original cook raw and without salt.

Yet the redoubtable Licinia is as nothing compared to the hazards involved in dealing with Marcus Manidus himself. Manidus, as the spice trader has discovered to his cost, is as mild-mannered a shark as any that has taken a massive bite out of an unsuspecting merchant's profits. He'll blink at you in that self-effacing way of his – then before you know it, you have bullied him into renting warehouse space to you at ten per cent above the going rate, and you have forced him to lock in those terms by signing an iron-clad contract.

Miyrius recalls going home feeling satisfied and slightly guilty of taking advantage of Manidus' gentle nature. Then, later that night, he had woken up to the realization of exactly what he had signed.

Yet Miyrius of Mira has no choice but to return to bargain with Manidus again – though this time, when they have shaken hands on the deal, he will be careful to count his fingers afterwards. He has just got word that the merchantman *Io's Child* has docked at Ostia. The *Child* is a typical ship of the time: a 75-tonner that carries some 1,500 *amphorae*. Among those *amphorae* are a dozen tightly stoppered containers with the little lead seal that marks them as the property of Miyrius the spice trader.

The containers are somewhat oddly shaped in comparison to the usual Roman *amphora*, for the simple reason that they are *not* the usual Roman *amphora*. They come from Barace, an almost unknown city on the west coast of India. Six of the containers are packed with cinnamon, incense and ginger, and – worth almost as much as the trading ship that carries them – the other six with finely ground black pepper.

These market towns [on the Indian coast] are frequently visited by large merchant vessels seeking great quantities of pepper and malabathrum [a plant rather like cinnamon].

There's also a lot here that is imported, such as bullion, topaz, fine cloth and linen, antimony, coral, crude glass, copper, tin, lead, wine ... and wheat to victual the ships, since the traders here do not supply it.

The exports include pepper, since there is one region here, a place called Cottonara, that supplies all the local markets. Other exports include an abundance of fine pearls, ivory, silk cloth, spikenard from the Ganges, malabathrum from the interior, and precious stones of all kinds including diamonds and sapphires.

Those travelling to this place from Egypt do so most favourably in Epiphi, which is the month of July.

Periplus of the Red Sea 56

Pepper is fantastically expensive – it would cost a workman half a month's wages to buy a single pound of it. However, the Romans like their food spicy, even though many of their spices – including pepper – have to be imported from outside the empire. Most Romans have no idea of the origins of the black powder that puts a kick into their lentil soup, but Miyrius knows that the stuff comes from Kerala in India. (There, the locals call the pepper *kari*, and 'curry' will be the name for spicy eastern dishes ever after.) Almost every recipe of the Roman cookery book writer Apicius contains pepper, yet for many dishes it is by far the most expensive ingredient.

Rome pays for pepper and other spices in gold, and sometimes

Miyrius wonders if it is entirely prudent to be shipping literally tons of gold out of the economy every year to pay for a luxury that vanishes into the imperial sewers hours after it is consumed. As the naturalist Pliny the Elder had remarked a century previously:

> *What's to recommend about pepper apart from a certain pungency? Other than that it is inferior to any fruit or berry. Yet, for this one desirable quality we import it all the way from India! ... Both pepper and ginger grow wild in their native countries, and yet here we buy them by weight – just as if we were measuring out gold or silver.*

Pliny Natural History 12.14.7

When you are importing materials as valuable as pepper to as venal a city as Rome, the one overwhelming requirement is to keep it in as safe a storage place as can be found. This is why Miyrius is going out to dinner tonight. Not only does his host Manidus own a warehouse secure against thieves who might break in from outside, but the staff of Manidus are famously unbribeable. Miyrius has seen too many valuable jars of spice 'evaporate' from locked rooms, or turn up with crudely tampered seals and filled with garbage. Manidus costs the earth, but at least goods come out of his warehouse in the same condition as that in which they entered.

When inviting Miyrius to dinner, Licinia had cunningly added that, as a merchant, Miyrius might be interested in one of their guests – a traveller who had been all the way to Cyrene and would recount his adventures while at the table. *Puh-lease!* Miyrius talks to no one about his travels, yet as a young man he voyaged far to set up the contacts that would later make his fortune. A traveller from Cyrene, indeed! As though a voyage to a minor city on the North African coast counted as an epic adventure. Miyrius knows that the world is large, far larger than the average Roman imagines, let alone the citizens of the imperial city itself, who appear to think that civilization stops at the municipal marker stones.

He remembers standing on a beach in Taprobane (which others will later call Serendib, Ceylon or Sri Lanka). He was talking to a sailor who was amazed to find himself so far west, far from his home port of Cattigara in Borneo on the Sinus Magnus, a huge body of ocean that the sailor called the 'South China Sea'. Miyrius told the sailor of yet more distant Gaul and Britain, and rumours of lands lying even further west, and the sailor had listened with polite scepticism.

SPICES ON THE MOVE. TRADERS AND CAMEL ON A BAS RELIEF

←————————————————————————————————→

Taprobane … was long looked upon as another world: the age and the arms of Alexander the Great were the first to give satisfactory proof that it is an island. Onesicritus, the commander of his fleet, has informed us that the elephants of this island are larger, and better adapted for warfare, than those of India; and from Megasthenes we learn that it is divided by a river, that the inhabitants have the name of Paleogoni, and that their country is more productive of gold and pearls of great size than even India.

PLINY *Natural History* 6.24 (John Bostock trans.)

←————————————————————————————————→

In turn, the sailor had told some tall tales of his own, of roads in imperial China greater than any of the Roman roads that Miyrius had described so proudly, roads so large that a special lane was reserved for imperial functionaries and messengers. When Miyrius had enquired sceptically as to why so great an empire had not made contact with Rome, he was told that the Chinese had indeed made repeated efforts. Every time, these attempted contacts had been vigorously blocked by the Parthian people of western Asia, who profited far too much from the trade along the Silk Road to want anyone to cut out the middleman.

That had been almost two decades ago. Miyrius had set out from Syria in the spring. He had first stopped at the Arabian port of Muza, where – in accordance with his father's orders – he secured long-term contracts for the import of perfumes and frankincense. Then, on his own initiative, he had travelled further, arriving at Ocelis just at the rising of the star some call the Soul of Isis, and others Sirius, the Dog Star.

Ocelis is the main embarkation point for those taking passage to India. The young Miyrius had been fortunate, for the wind they call Hippalus picked up as he arrived and the ships of the trading fleet were setting off on their annual voyage. Within a month, Miyrius was drinking wine with merchants in Muziris, a city on India's western coast. From here he travelled by road to the lands of a people called the Neacindi. The main port here is at the mouth of a river – important to Miyrius, because pepper is shipped downriver from the interior. According to the traders with whom he spoke, the inland pepper farmers hollowed out logs in the manner of dugout canoes, packed them with their precious cargo, and floated downriver to sell their produce at the port.

Antun [Antoninus] the ruler of Daquin [Rome] sent envoys beyond the frontiers who reached us via Rinan [Vietnam] … This was our first [direct] contact with them.

Hou Hanshu Chronicle AD 166

Like all long-distance traders, Miyrius knows the ratios 1:5:28. The first is the cost of shipping an amphora by sea on an established trading route. It is five times cheaper than moving that amphora the same distance by river barge, and twenty-eight times cheaper than moving the goods overland by ox-cart. That's why it is cheaper to import corn from Egypt than to trek it over the Apennines from the Po valley in Northern Italy.

Since 246 BC, a canal has connected the Red Sea to the Nile, and from the Nile goods flow downriver to the great city of Alexandria, and from there to the rest of Rome's empire. Miyrius returned along this route with his first ever cargo of pepper and spices, sailing in late December with the south-east winds, and arriving at his father's emporium in Syria just over a year after he had set out.

And now, at dinner, he was to hear of a trip to Cyrene as though it were a voyage to the ends of the earth. Yet it is from the true ends of the earth that the spices at their table will come, and even Miyrius wonders where those ends might actually lie.

For the travellers from the seas around Java spoke of lands yet much more distant to the south and east. Other merchants talk of a lost city somewhere in the great African desert, and beyond that a mighty black river ('Niger' meaning 'black' in Latin), which might be a branch of the Nile, but probably isn't. Miyrius has a friend in Pompeii whose house boasts a statue that he claims came from north-east India, and another who has a curiously wrought amulet from Thule, 'six days' travel, sailing north of Britain to the borders of the frozen sea' (Strabo's *Geography* 1.4). A remarkable place this Thule must be, for, as Pliny says, 'when the sun passes through the sign of Cancer there can be no night at all, just as in midwinter there would be no day'.

←——————————————————————————→

The Phoenicians departed from Egypt by way of the Erythraean [Red Sea], and from there to the southern ocean. Every autumn, they went ashore wherever they had ended up, and sowed corn. They waited until it was ready to harvest and having done so, they sailed on.

This they did for two whole years, and on the third year they came home through the Pillars of Hercules [Straits of Gibraltar], and so completed their voyage. When they returned they swore that when they rounded the southernmost point of Lybia [i.e. Africa] the noon sun was on their right. I for one do not believe this.[14]

HERODOTUS *History* Bk 4

←——————————————————————————→

The world is huge and strange, and only merchants in their quest for new trade routes and goods have probed – unsuccessfully – to find its limits. Sometimes Miyrius wonders if the gods who allegedly gave the Romans their 'empire without limit' realize that they were actually bestowing on the Romans a relatively small chunk of land on the shores of a somewhat minor sea.

Miyrius considers this as he walks up the Caelian Hill along the Street of the Sandal-makers, the craftsmen's stalls shuttered and still in the early evening. Behind him tramp two of his stolid employees, part bodyguards and part torchbearers, who will light the trip home for him. One carries in a bundle the *synthesis*, or dining suit, into which Miyrius will change when he has reached his destination. After all, while the toga is the usual formal Roman attire, it needs to be elaborately wrapped around the body and held in place by a crooked elbow. The whole thing has nary a buckle or knot, which makes it totally unsuitable for dining.

Yet the Romans do not like the sight of naked flesh in public and so have come up with the *synthesis*, a colourful set of clothes easily put together before a meal (which is why anything artificially put together in later ages will be called 'synthetic'). While only someone as decadent as the former emperor Nero would actually wear a synthesis as his daily attire, as evening wear the garments are a good way of displaying wealth and status. That of Miyrius, for example, is in saffron-coloured silk with purple dragons embroidered on the hems – thus advertising his access to the wealth and treasures of the east.

Because this garment is so valuable, Miyrius is alert for suspicious movement on the street. As a result, his eye is immediately drawn to the hooded figure skulking on the pavement opposite. If ever a man were lurking with intent, it is this fellow. However, he is evidently waiting for Miyrius to move out of sight before fulfilling his nefarious purpose, rather than targeting Miyrius himself. The spice merchant gives the man one last curious stare before heading onwards to his business meal and the inevitable fleecing that awaits at the hands of the soft-eyed and flint-hearted Manidus.

⚏ HORA NOCTIS II ⚏
(20.00–21.00)

THE PROSTITUTE
FINDS A CLIENT

Anyone who believes that young men should be forbidden from intercourse with prostitutes, he is indeed a morally austere character! ... He is also at variance with the morality of both the past and present ... For when was this not done? Who ever criticized it, who objected?

CICERO *Pro Caelio* 20

Mamila had never before thought she would miss her room at the Lupara Larentia. The brothel at which she usually works and lives is named after the (in)famous Acca Larentia. This lady was a contemporary of Romulus, the founder of Rome, and indeed by some accounts she was the founder's adoptive mother. After a career spent entertaining the great and good of the era, including Hercules (though, in fact, few contemporary woman seem to have escaped that fate), Larentia married well. After a happy old age she died and left her substantial fortune to the Roman people. Her memory is still celebrated in a festival, the Larentina, every 23 December.

It is also the ideal of Mamila to marry well and escape her current life. However, she is aware that this is an ambition that she shares with practically every other woman in the swarms of prostitutes who frequent the city. Consequently, the pool of potential husbands has been pretty much hunted to extinction. In any case, Mamila has only the vaguest idea of what constitutes regular Roman family life. The brothel is the only home she really remembers. Like many a Roman streetwalker, Mamila was 'adopted' at birth – and in this case, 'adopted' means picked off the street where she had been abandoned as a newborn infant, and reared by brothel workers.

Rome practices what has been rather brutally called 'post-natal birth control', by which unwanted children like Mamila are literally thrown out with the garbage. The unlucky ones get torn apart by feral dogs, luckier ones are picked up for rearing as slave servants, and the luckiest of all are quietly adopted into the household of a childless couple who pretend it was their baby all along.

Between the ages of two and five, Mamila did spend some time in a well-off household. She was rented by the brothel that had 'adopted' her to be a *delicata*, a combination of human pet and companion to the couple's legitimate daughter. However, the same tempestuous disposition that has led to Mamila walking the streets this evening also led to her being deemed an unsuitable member of her adoptive household.

Thereafter, Mamila was returned to the brothel from which she had been hired out to the family. For the next few years she grew up as an *ancilla ornatrice*. That is, a girl who helps to clean up and fix the hair of the house prostitutes after each amorous engagement, and who also occasionally fortifies them with a beaker of unwatered wine in readiness for the next encounter. As a sort of substitute daughter for the women working at the establishment, Mamila did not find life too bad. She simply took it for granted that, as soon as the *villicus puellarum* (who looked after the girls of the brothel) agreed with the doctor that she was *viripotens* (capable of handling a man) she would be given her own room and take up regular employment.

Things did not work out that way for, before she could start at the brothel, there was some sort of disturbance. Perhaps the owner had failed to bribe the local gangsters, or had fallen out with the city magistrates. All Mamila remembered was burly men with clubs smashing the premises and beating and raping the girls. She had fled, and found herself alone on the street. Quickly, she turned to the only livelihood she knew, making a dangerous living as an unlicensed prostitute. (What happened to her original owners, Mamila has no idea. She has been careful not to find out, since she has regarded herself as a free woman ever since she fled her previous establishment.)

Generally speaking, a woman who intends to work as a prostitute does so by going to the city Aediles, and giving her name, age and place of birth. She then picks a pseudonym that will be her working name, since most families prefer that a working girl abandons her original family name. The Aedile then gives the woman her licence, and makes a rough assessment of what she should charge. (This is not free advice – it's because she is expected to pay tax on that amount per customer.)

---

*He [Caligula] was first to put a tax on the earnings of prostitutes
as a percentage of what each earned for a session, and he added a
clause that all those who had ever been prostitutes should pay this
even if they were now married.*

SUETONIUS *Life of Caligula* 40

The historian Tacitus remarked with outraged horror the story
of an aristocratic woman called Visitilia who, facing punishment
for her numerous affairs, evaded the law by simply applying for a
prostitute's licence (*licentia stupri*). When the Aediles could find no
reason not to give it to her, she carried on as she had before, but now
charged for it.

While many working-class Romans regard licensed prostitution
as simply another career choice, the life of an unregistered girl is
marginal at best. She has to compete with the cheapest of legal
streetwalkers, and most of these perform for little more than a loaf
of bread and a measure of wine. Therefore, Mamila regards herself
as fortunate that she met Syricus, an evil little whippet of a man.
After careful negotiations, the pair formed a partnership. Mamila
would lure marks into alleyways or quiet alcoves, and there her
would-be clients were relieved of their purses, clothes and anything
else of value at the point of Syricus' dagger.

Mamila had the sense to realize that the life of a *galina* – as
these robber-prostitutes are called – tends to finish messily, either
in some anonymous alleyway, or dramatically in the arena (the
magistrates like to get sadistically creative when making an example
of condemned women in her profession). Even while profiting from
the proceeds of crime, Mamila was planning her escape.

A PROSTITUTE DROPS HER TOGA IN THIS MOSAIC SCENE

Lucius [in the form of a donkey] is appalled at the prospect of having public sex with a woman:

A soldier ran to get the woman from her cell. As I said earlier, she had been condemned for her many crimes, and was to be thrown to wild beasts after copulating with me. For that purpose a couch was being prepared, richly decorated with tortoiseshell from India, a feather mattress and a flowery silk coverlet.

It was bad enough that I must shame myself by publicly having sex with that filthy woman. But I was also in fear of my own life. Once we were locked in the embrace of Venus, what savage animal would they unleash to devour the woman? Whatever it was, it would hardly be so well trained and uncommonly gentle as to rip into her and spare the innocent beast locked between her thighs.

APULEIUS *The Golden Ass*, bk 10

Carefully hoarding her ill-gotten gains, Mamila managed to ditch Syricus (by some reports he is still looking for her), changed her name and officially registered with the authorities. Thereafter, she rented a room at the Lupara Larentia on the other side of town. 'Room' is putting it rather strongly – actually, what Mamila has is a cramped, windowless nook with a curtain separating it from the main hallway. Next to the curtain is a small sign that gives her name, price, and specialities. On the back is written the single word 'busy'. As a customer enters the alcove, he flips the sign so that others know they must wait their turn.

Mamila's cubicle has a bed of solid concrete, and a compensatingly thick mattress, covered with a blanket that, for obvious reasons, is changed frequently. The thing about the room that Mamila likes least is the lack of ventilation. As a result, she constantly smells of the smoke from her oil lamp, despite frequent visits to the baths. (A fringe benefit of her job is that because she is not respectable, Mamila is not banned from the baths when men are present. Not only can she bathe at any time of day, but usually earns her entrance fee within fifteen minutes of arrival.)

It's not the life she would have chosen, but until last night Mamila would have reckoned she was getting by. True, her good intentions about saving for old age seem to melt away in the presence of *amorges* dresses or Arabian perfumes, but she had steady employment, a loyal client base and most of her life ahead of her.

The Floralia [Festival of the Goddess Flora] was solemnized with every kind of wantonness. The prostitutes used their freedom of speech to give vent to every kind of obscenity and, urged on by the rabble, they strip off their clothing. Then they act as mimes, holding the crowd fascinated with their wriggling buttocks.

LACTANTIUS *Institutiones Divinae* 20, 6.

Then Mancinus, that fool of an Aedile, had to come pounding on her door after midnight. Mamila does not regret hurling the flowerpot at the magistrate's head, and is, in fact, secretly proud of her steady hand and good aim. However, she does very much regret that her impetuous act has resulted in her being suspended from the brothel until her court appearance next week.

EROTIC ROMAN OIL LAMP

Thereafter, if Mancinus' threat comes to fruition, Mamila will be sentenced to serve as a slave among the camp followers of the Roman army. This is a life of drudgery and continual use of her services, which is then interrupted by moments of pure terror when the troops are in action. Camp followers are the last to be fed, and the first to be abandoned if danger threatens. Basically, it is the equivalent of the slave mines to which a man might be sentenced.

Therefore, over the next week Mamila will be working as a *nonaria,* a 'ninth-hour girl'. That's the term for prostitutes who work the street and are only allowed to practise after most people have finished work at the ninth hour (3 p.m.). By applying herself, it is her hope to afford enough to visit a jurist and explore her options as to how to present a defence to the judge.

Which is why she is currently kicking herself for having drifted over to the base of the Caelian Hill. The hill itself is a bastion of respectability (or, at least, the people who live thereabouts can afford their own slave concubines, which amounts to the same thing as being respectable). The base is ringed with workmen who make their living from the patronage of those living higher up the hill, and most of these workmen's stalls are closed for the night. Customers are few. At the same time, there's no point in moving on to the Subarra, or the Cariniae at the foot of the Esquiline Hill. That area is packed with brothels, taverns and freelancers, and frankly, Mamila prefers less competition.

A man got his slave pregnant. At the birth, his father suggested that the child be killed. The genius replied, 'Kill your own child and then tell me to murder mine.'

PHILOGELOS 57

She is wondering whether to move down towards the Colosseum to see if she can pick up any trade around the fountain, or perhaps at the foot of the gigantic statue of the sun god that gives the area its name. (The arches – *fornes* – of the massive arena that dominates the Colosseum area are themselves so popular with prostitutes that they are said to be the origin of the word 'fornication'.) However, Mamila stops her wandering at the sight of a small party moving along the Street of the Sandal-makers.

No, it's a bust. It looks like a group on their way to a social occasion, and, at this hour, they are running late in any case. The well-dressed Asiatic type who is evidently the leader of the group gives her a single glance and instantly dismisses her from his mind. The attendants following also ignore her and fix their gaze instead on an odd-looking pair on the other side of the street.

One is a cloaked figure who is very conspicuously trying to avoid attention. The other is a muscular-looking thug who actually has avoided attention by casually stepping behind a street kiosk and then stopping there. The hooded man waits miserably under the party's scrutiny until the dinner party has proceeded on its way, and then he looks around nervously for the thug. But by this time the thug has seen Mamila, and the pair exchange a slow stare of mutual appreciation and evaluation.

If you want a good screw, look for Attice. She's only 16 copper coins.

POMPEIAN GRAFFITO, *Corpus Inscriptiones Latinarum* 4.17.61

It's not as though it is hard to discover what Mamila is doing there. She's not as blatant as the *dorides* (women who stand naked at the doors of some brothels and taverns to lure in passers-by), but she *is* wearing a toga. On a Roman man, the toga is a symbol of respectability. On a Roman woman of negotiable virtue, the toga is a highly practical garment without fastenings that a) drops to the ground after a practised wiggle of the shoulders, and b) when on the ground, the garment – which is actually a semi-circle of thick woven wool – forms a soft blanket for what happens next.

The hooded man follows the thug's gaze and says something irritably. Reluctantly, the thug moves on, with Mamila tagging hopefully along some forty paces behind. The hooded figure stops at a small doorway set into an otherwise featureless wall. After a furtive look around that even attracts the attention of the pigeons that are the only other occupants of the street, the hooded man slips through the doorway. As he does so, he mutters something to the thug, and there is the glint of silver changing hands.

Mamila stands her ground, grinning impudently as the thug approaches.

Blondie has taught me to hate dark-haired girls, so hate them I shall – as best I can. I'd prefer to love them instead. Venus Fisica wrote this.

GRAFFITI ON THE WALL OF THE ATRIUM OF A POMPEIAN BROTHEL,
Corpus Inscriptiones Latinarum 6.14.43 1520

'Hey, big boy. Got something for me?'

The helmet-scarred forehead, the over-muscled torso – either he's an ex-soldier who has taken up weights, or he's a gladiator.

The gladiator's interest is evident, and not just in his expression. He holds out his hand, showing coins worth a day's wages.

'My client says to give you these and you forget that you ever saw him here.'

As Mamila reaches for the money, the gladiator playfully snatches his hand away. 'Nuh-uh. You want it, you have to earn it. I'm supposed to be watching that door over there, but I reckon we'll still have a good view in that side street. Deal?'

Without waiting for a reply, he casually picks up Mamila and tucks her under his arm like a bundle of washing. He heads determinedly for the shadowy service road, and Mamila's dislodged toga trails behind them like a wedding gown.

Mamila appealed to the Tribunes of the Plebs, declaring that Mancinus had come to her in party clothes and had tried to break in … The tribunes decided that if he [Mancinus] had been as a party-goer he had been justly treated; if he had been there as a magistrate, it was not proper that he be there at all.

AULUS GELLIUS *NA* 4.14

☷ HORA NOCTIS III ☷
(21.00–22.00)

THE ASTROLOGER CASTS
A HOROSCOPE

Always consider the universe as a single living entity, with one
form and one soul. Observe how everything has reference to
one perception, the perception of this one living thing. See how
all things act with one movement; and how all things are the
interacting cause of everything else. See how the web of life is thus
formed in thread and texture.

MARCUS AURELIUS *Meditations* 4,40

As his client enters the room, the astrologer Balbilus is tempted
to bury his head in his hands. How is it that this Ofella, the man
who is generally known as a master intriguer, the ruthless fixer for
the powerful Lucius Ceionius Commodus, master of the Roman

senate, can be so bad at actual cloak-and-dagger work?

Did he, Balbilus wonders, actually carry a sign that proclaimed 'I swear I am up to no good', as he skulked so conspicuously through the streets of Rome? Balbilus hopes not, because the last thing he wants is word of tonight's consultation to get out. What he and Ofella will do tonight might be construed as high treason, for they will be trying to discover when and how the emperor Hadrian will die.

(Not that Hadrian himself does not know this already. The emperor is meant to be so expert an astrologer that every year on the *kalends* of January, he actually writes down everything that will happen to him over the coming year. Indeed, it is rumoured that he has on record what he will be doing right at the hour of his death.)

Obviously, emperors are not keen on the general public knowing when they are predicted to die, lest senior politicians who are enemies decide that this is an auspicious moment to make sure they really do. Therefore, casting an imperial horoscope tends to be terminally discouraged. However, there are those such as this client, a relatively minor senator, for whom knowing when there will be a change of ruler is not a matter of political expedience but of simple survival. As well as the horoscope of the emperor, Balbilus has also been paid a small fortune to cast the horoscopes of Ofella's patron Lucius Ceionius Commodus and his fiercest rival, Pedanius Fuscus Salinator. What Ofella is paying for, in short, is a description of what will happen when Hadrian dies, and who will succeed him.

←—————————————————————————→

A certain fortuneteller warned Caesar that he would be in great danger on that day in March which the Romans call the Ides. When that day dawned and Caesar was on his way to the senate house, he happened to notice the seer, and jokingly called to him, 'See, the Ides of March have come.'

'Aye,' muttered the seer, 'but not yet gone.'

PLUTARCH *Life of Caesar* 63

←——————————————————————————→

Momentarily, Balbilus is distracted by recalling a popular joke: a woman goes to an astrologer and asks him to cast the horoscope of her sick son. On being assured that the lad has a long and prosperous life ahead of him, the woman gratefully promises to pay the astrologer the next day. 'Pay now,' says the astrologer. 'Just in case.'

Although it actually has nothing to do with astrology, Balbilus believes he can predict with some certainty that the emperor Hadrian is on his way out, and the cause will be heart disease. He was in the crowd a few years back when the emperor had dedicated the temple of Venus and Rome. By chance, Hadrian had passed close enough for the astrologer to note a transverse crease in the imperial earlobe. Balbilus has a similar crease in his own ear, and family experience reports that those with this marking tend to die early of congestive heart failure. Given the stresses that his career put upon an emperor (so far, eight of Rome's twelve emperors have died either violently or under highly suspicious circumstances) one can assume that even a healthy imperial heart would be subject to a degree of stress. If Hadrian has even a slight coronary defect, then his fate is written on his earlobe rather than in the stars.

Ofella is eager to get started on the chart. He has set a gladiator to guard the door to ensure there are no distractions, and now that he has shown his hand he wants the entire business done and forgotten as soon as possible. The first issue – and the roadblock that has held up the conspirators for the past week – is that the canny Hadrian has no intention of making it easy for those wanting to cast his horoscope. As a result, no one is exactly sure of when or where he was born.

By very discreet enquiry, Ofella has discovered that the emperor celebrates his birthday on 24 January, and that his birth took place in the year 829 AUC (*Ab urbe condita* – the years since the founding of the city of Rome) or AD 76 in later reckoning. This means that the Sun was in Aquarius, and Hadrian has the dominant signs of Aquarius, Capricorn and Pisces with ruling planets of Uranus and the Sun. So far, so good, but the angle of the moon in the ascendant is determined by the place of birth, and while some say that this was in Italica in Spain, others insist that the birth actually happened in Rome. Naturally, Hadrian is in no hurry to clear up the confusion, and his agents are rather persistent in asking for the exact reasons why the enquirer wants to know such details.

In the end, Balbilus decided that the easiest thing to do is to cast two horoscopes, one for each location, and to optimistically assume that Hadrian is not being deceptive about his birth date.

Another popular joke pops treacherously into the astrologer's mind:

While travelling abroad, a young man visits an astrologer, seeking information on how his family is doing during his absence. After checking the young man's star dates, the astrologer confidently informs him that all is well back home, and his mother and father are thriving.

'Hold on,' says the young man. 'My father's been dead for these last fifteen years.'

The astrologer consults the chart again and sympathetically says to the youth, 'You have no idea who your real father is, have you?'

Augustus was
a Capricorn

The Balbilus family

The first Balbilus was the son of the noted astrologer Thrasyllus, who was a friend of the emperor Tiberius. Tiberius was once about to throw Thrasyllus off a cliff for predicting future success while he remained a miserable exile. However, Thrasyllus pointed to a ship, and correctly predicted that it bore news of Tiberius' restoration to Rome.

The son of Thrasyllus was court astrologer to Claudius, Nero and Vespasian. After serving these three very different emperors, he wrote a treatise on astrology, of which fragments survive. Seneca, the philosopher and man of letters, described him as 'a man of esoteric learning'. Balbilus died in Ephesus around the time Hadrian was born.

His daughter was called Claudia Capitolina, and if she had given birth to a son, this would be the Balbilus described here.

In other words, garbage in, garbage out, and Balbilus has no idea of the accuracy of the information he is using to calculate Hadrian's future. He does know that the job has been done before – Hadrian learned his astrological skills from his paternal uncle Aelius, who was considered one of the great experts of his day. He let on that the horoscope of Hadrian fulfilled the main preconditions of an imperial horoscope in which:

> *The epicentric Sun and the Moon were equally served by five other planets. Above all, the Sun and the Moon are located in the essential key points: that is, in the Horoscopic Point or in the Mesouranema, and they are thus served by all the planets. Consequently, these aspects cause those who are born under such a conjunction to become kings ruling over many nations.*

> FRAGMENT FROM THE *Astronomica* of Antigonus of Nicea

Having an uncle whose divinations reveal that one has an imperial horoscope is certainly a mixed blessing. When one Vettius Pompustius discovered that he had an imperial horoscope, he regarded this as an amusing oddity until the unamused emperor of the day (Domitian) had him executed, just in case.

Perhaps a more sensible approach was that of Domitian's father, Vespasian. When informers brought him news of a senator whose horoscope (wrongly) foretold he would be emperor, Vespasian did not have the man killed. Instead, he gifted the man with a large estate. When his son asked what Vespasian thought he was playing at, the wily old emperor replied, 'It would appear to be necessary that one day this man should owe us a large favour.'

As Balbilus works through his numbers, he hits another snag.

Ofella, it turns out, is a backseat astrologer. After the two have quibbled over several interpretations of the data, a theological divide is revealed. Ofella follows the teachings of Ptolemy of Egypt. Ptolemy is doubtless a great astrologer, whose works will determine the course of astrology in future ages. His epic works – the *Almagest* and the *Tetrabiblos* – are destined to last for centuries, if not millennia, so well do they explain celestial phenomena and their interpretation.

Claudius Ptolemy

Born in Egypt on an unknown date, Ptolemy did his best work in the early second century. He probably based his mathematics on the work of one Theon of Smyrna and, furthermore, had access to the wealth of material in the great library of Alexandria.

His work called the *Almagest* was actually not so called in Rome, as this term comes from a translation from Greek to Arabic, and only in the Middle Ages was this translated into Latin. Along with Euclid's *Elements of Geometry*, it is one of the longest-lasting scientific texts.

So well did Ptolemy describe the astronomical phenomena of his day that his theory that the earth was the centre of the universe survived until the invention of the telescope. These days, a 'Ptolemaic Universe' is used to describe a theory that accounts for all the known data while still being completely wrong.

However, Ptolemy is a recent phenomenon who has burst on to the astrological scene. While he has picked up flocks of followers, such as the annoying Ofella, many of the professionals such as Balbilus prefer to work with the system of Marcus Manilius, whose work predates Ptolemy by several generations. The Balbilus family have been astrologers for all that time, and one reason why Ofella has chosen to consult with Balbilus is because it is rumoured that Manilius personally passed on to Balbilus' great-grandfather Thrasyllus the Great Secret: how, through astrology, the span of a man's life might be calculated.

'But Ptolemy has made astrology a science,' Ofella argues. 'Just look at his mathematical formulae.'

'The Manilian system worked for Domitian,' counters Balbilus.

There is a pause, and the pair reflect upon the relationship of the late, unlamented emperor Domitian and the contemporary astrologers of his empire. There was, for example, the case of the astrologer Ascletario. This man, an initiate into the Great Secret, made no pretence that he did not know the future. Brought before the emperor, he admitted that he had checked to see what his own fate would be. His corpse, he said, would be torn apart by dogs – and that this would happen very soon. Domitian reasoned that if the man himself thought he was soon to die, he should be proven right. If not, he anyway deserved death for being an impudent charlatan.

Accordingly, he had the man executed. But he ordered that, rather than be thrown to the dogs, the corpse should be buried with full honours. Later, while the emperor was at dinner, one guest mentioned a strange incident – a funeral pyre had been toppled by a sudden gale and before the attendants could stop them, feral dogs had torn apart the corpse of the deceased – who was an astrologer called Ascletario.

Domitian was also disturbed by a prophecy that, 'There will be blood on the moon as she enters Aquarius, and a deed will be done for everyone to talk about throughout the entire world.' Starting the night before his death, the moon was indeed blood-red – as can happen if the wind from the south whips dust from the Sahara into the upper atmosphere. The problem, as the astrologically aware Domitian well knew, was that on this occasion the moon was due to enter Aquarius at the fifth hour of that very day.

This, together with other signs and portents, let Domitian know the exact hour of his forthcoming death. Come the hour, and the emperor waited nervously, surrounded by supposedly loyal guards. Eventually, he asked the time. As arranged, his freedmen untruthfully reported that it was the sixth hour. Relieved that the hour foretold for his death had come and gone, Domitian went off quickly and happily to prepare for a bath – and there in the bedroom he encountered his assassin, exactly on schedule.

For the Manilian system to work best, the astrologer needs not just the exact time and place of birth, but also the time of conception, for as the great man himself remarks:

The fates rule the world, and all things are established by a settled law; each long age is marked with its settled fortune. At our birth we begin to die, and our end depends upon our beginning.

Unlike Ptolemy, who prefers to do his divinations principally by sun signs, the followers of Manilius tend to give equal importance to the moon and the rising sign. This is why, in the decades before the Ptolemaic system took hold, many leading Romans took as their astrological sign one different from their sun sign. For example, the emperor Augustus (born 23 September) was – according to

Ptolemy – a Libran. Yet Augustus considered himself a Capricorn. Those with a Capricorn ascendant are good managers, competent, image-conscious and driven. They often have a difficult childhood, such as coping with illness, being the protégé of Julius Caesar and having to survive his assassination.

In his retirement at Apollonia, he went with his friend Agrippa to visit Theogenes, the astrologer, in his gallery on the roof. Agrippa, who first consulted the fates, having great and almost incredible fortunes predicted of him; Augustus did not choose to make known his nativity, and persisted for some time in the refusal, from a mixture of shame and fear, lest his fortunes should be predicted as inferior to those of Agrippa.

Being persuaded, however, after much importunity, to declare it, Theogenes started up from his seat, and paid him adoration. Not long afterwards, Augustus was so confident of the greatness of his destiny, that he published his horoscope.

SUETONIUS *Life of Augustus* 92 (trans. Alexander Thomson ed.)

Hadrian, born on 24 January (allegedly), is an Aquarius. Therefore, as one might expect of a man who has architecture as a hobby and likes to experiment with domes, this Aquarian is interested in technology. Those with his birth date are supposedly highly intelligent (Hadrian is a polymath) and somewhat insecure (Hadrian has a habit of suddenly turning on friends he thinks may have betrayed him). As his birthdate is paired with air, Hadrian is inclined to travel – so far to Britain, Africa, Asia Minor and Egypt. His birthdate is linked with spiritual and psychic ability.

'Yes, yes,' mutters Ofella, 'but when will he *die*?'

Well, thinks Balbilus, it's probably heart failure that will kill the emperor. Now, Aries rules the head, Taurus rules the neck, Libra the groin and Cancer the chest. Now, the heart is in the chest and the sign of Cancer is from 21 June–22 July ... so, looking at the position of Jupiter, the ruler of planets and the alignment of the sun with Aquarius ...

'July. As far as my abilities tell me, the emperor will be dead on or soon before the Ides [15] of July.'

After this, Hadrian left [Rome] for [the seaside resort of] Baiae. [The future emperor] Antoninus was left to govern in Rome. But Hadrian's condition remained critical, and so he sent for Antoninus, and died in his presence on the sixth day before the Ides of July.

HADRIAN, *Historia Augusta*, 25

THE GLADIATOR STRUTS
HIS STUFF

Life is good for Sergius the gladiator. It is also remarkably simple. An unkind colleague once remarked that the main purpose of Sergius' brain is to keep his ears apart, but this is not entirely true. It is just that, for Sergius, life is mostly about fighting, fornication and finding someone to pay for it.

Just as he is seldom short of willing bedmates, it is never hard for Sergius to get into a fight. He has been trained within an inch of his life (and knows of several deceased trainees who were trained an inch past that) at gladiator school. This school is an unforgiving place, where the *lanista* (gladiator trainer) can club, whip or brand his charges, and, as did every gladiator who signs up at the school, Sergius has sworn the Gladiator's Oath '*uri, vinciri, verberari, ferroque necari*' ('I will submit to being burned, bound and beaten.

I may be killed by the sword').

It is a brutal trade. A trainee who fails to shape up might even be matched against a more proficient rival simply to give the other practice at killing. And yet, even though he's no longer compelled to do so, Sergius still attends that school, and while he is there he takes the opportunity to train as though his life depends upon it – because it does.

Ave Caesar

'Ave Caesar, moriaturi te salutant!' This is the famous greeting which many assume started every gladiator fight. Except it didn't. As far as we know the term was only used once. That was when, to celebrate the conclusion of public works on the (now drained) Fucine Lake, the emperor Claudius staged a mock naval battle (for a given value of 'mock' battle – for the participants it was a very real struggle indeed).

The assembled prisoners greeted Claudius with the now famous 'Hail Caesar! Those about to die salute you', to which Claudius replied cryptically, 'Aut non' ('Or not'). He did, though, spare many of the survivors afterwards.

However, after this one usage, by fighters who were not properly gladiators anyway, this famous greeting by the doomed was apparently never used again.

CF SUETONIUS *Life of Claudius* 21

Sergius is an *auctoratus*. This means that while most gladiators fight because they have no choice, Sergius is a gladiator because he wants to be. Originally condemned to fight in the arena as punishment for banditry, five years ago Sergius briefly gained fame in the Colosseum when he slew a well-known opponent. Wisely, he invested the money he earned from that bout to buy himself out of his contract. His proudest possession is his *rudis*, the wooden sword that he received along with his freedom. This sword is proof that he has expunged his crime by his bravery, and though Sergius can never be a Roman citizen, the good life in Rome is his for the taking.

MOSAIC SHOWING GLADIATORS AT PRACTICE

However free he might be, a highly trained, six-foot slab of vertical muscle still needs employment. So Sergius continues to fight in the arena as a *murmillo*, a heavily armed gladiator who wields a legionary shield and uses a heavy stabbing sword the length of his forearm. Although he wears some armour while fighting, his pride and joy is his helmet – a wide-brimmed object of Thracian steel chased with gold scrollwork. A grille hides his face while he is in combat, and atop the helmet sits the wide crest like the fin of a fish (*mormylos*) that gives the *murmillo* his name. Embossed on Sergius' crest are scenes from the bout that earned him his reputation and his freedom.

So far, Sergius has fought once this year – and lost. Fortunately, only around one in five of all gladiator fights is fatal. This combat was part of the *Ludi Cerealia* in late April, and was fought with blunted swords. Gladiators are, after all, highly expensive investments and their owners (or in Sergius' case, agents) are loath to see them killed. However, when the emperor is sponsoring the games, or at the midwinter festival of the Saturnalia – when Sergius will fight next – it is a different story. Then, fights are to the death. In fact, before the bout the *editor*, who stages the Saturnalia games, will be presented with the swords of Sergius and his opponent so that he can check for himself that they are lethally sharp. Sergius is very much looking forward to the occasion, for it will be his return match with the *hoplomachus* (Greek-style) gladiator who humbled him last time.

Thumbs Down Means 'Spared'?

It's true that the Romans signalled the fate of a defeated gladiator with *pollice verso* (the 'turning of the thumb'). However, nowhere does it say in which direction the thumb is turned. Consider this. A doomed gladiator will steady himself by holding his opponent's knee, and will be killed by a downward strike through the neck.

So, hold an imaginary sword with which to stab downwards, and note where your thumb is. It points up. Now, instead of killing your opponent, sheath your sword – as the Romans did – on the opposite side of your body (i.e. if you are right-handed, sheath the sword on your left hip). Your thumb goes down.

Therefore, it may be that thumbs up signalled 'stab him' and thumbs down meant 'put the sword away'.

Two combats a year make up just under half the number that a full-time gladiator usually fights. This probably explains why, unlike most of his contemporaries, Sergius has survived into his thirties. Though he is paid a tidy sum for each bout – about the equivalent of a year's wages for a skilled artisan – Sergius has both expensive tastes and an unfortunate penchant for betting on the Blues in the chariot races. (Gambling is supposed to be illegal in Rome, but this barely affects Sergius, who has friends in both high and low places.)

Any gladiator knows what happens to a man who cannot pay his gambling debts, for like many of his colleagues Sergius has a profitable sideline in scientifically breaking the fingers, legs or kneecaps (according to specification) of defaulting debtors. Debt collection aside, Sergius also keeps his creditors happy with bodyguarding jobs. These are usually paid for by the hour by wealthy aristocrats who want bodyguards more to show off their importance than to protect them from actual danger. However, there are times – as with the job Sergius has just performed so poorly – when a clandestine meeting might have turned violent without the hulking shadow of a gladiator looming in the background.

Sergius has no idea what went on behind the door he was recently guarding. A smugglers' conclave, a treasonous cabal or turf negotiations between street gang leaders – Sergius has kept the peace at all of these and cared less about the proceedings than about his pay. With coin safely stowed in his purse, he hurries to his next gig – an aristocratic household on the Caelian Hill where dinner is just finishing.

A good host will finish a dinner party with an entertainment. Lascivious dancing girls from Gades, perhaps, or the titillating poems of Catullus recited by a pretty girl with a lyre. Some hosts prefer to show acrobats from Lycia in Asia Minor, and still others will stage a demonstration bout by real gladiators. Tonight's combat will be with wooden legionary training swords, so no one will die, though broken bones are possible and bruises a certainty. In anticipation of the event, Sergius has already stashed his gear at the client's house.

<hr>

Although he [Alypius] had utterly detested such spectacles, one day he happened to meet up with a crowd of friends and fellow students returning from dinner. With friendly violence, they dragged him kicking and screaming into the amphitheatre, on a day featuring one of those cruel and murderous shows.

He protested, 'You can drag in my body and sit me down here. But you can't make my eyes or mind focus on the spectacle. I will be absent while present'.

If only he had shut his ears also! One of the combatants fell in the fight, and the huge roar from the spectators stirred him so strongly that he was overwhelmed by curiosity... He opened his eyes and was struck more deeply in his soul than the victim had been wounded in his body... For, as soon as he saw the blood, his mind drank it in with a savage temper, and he did not turn away, but fixed his eyes on the bloody pastime. He soaked up the madness in delight with the wicked contest, drunk with blood lust.

AUGUSTINE *Confessions* 6.8

Sergius dons the wide *baletus* (a metal-studded leather belt that protects much of his abdomen) and a padded arm-cover that will help guard his sword arm against the blows of his opponent, a Thracian-style gladiator who will be using a lighter, curved sword, also of wood. The pair have a brief, grunted conversation before the bout. It is agreed they will spar for about fifteen minutes to give their patrons a show and then, well, let the best man win.

SERGIUS IN AGGRESSIVE POSE

Cheers greet the gladiators as they parade from the atrium to a torchlit walled garden at the back of the house. The host and his guests sit on chairs set up at the edge of the makeshift arena, and Sergius notices that the hostess sits eagerly in the front row, just as the Vestal Virgins do at the more deadly fights in the Colosseum. Slaves peek furtively from the windows of the kitchen, where the irritated chef occasionally clouts them back to their duties of preparing and serving post-dinner delicacies and snacks.

The Thracian is agile and skilled. He dances around the more ponderous Sergius, and lands a few playful whacks on his opponent's prized helmet. The spectators cheer or boo according to their bets, and gasp as Sergius takes a wicked blow to the kidneys. He has clearly been getting the worst of the fight before the Thracian signals that the time for sparring has elapsed by stabbing at Sergius' face with his curved sword. Sergius blocks by raising his shield, so that the sword passes over his shoulder. This clumsy parry is just what the Thracian wanted, as he can now drive the curved tip of his sword into his opponent's unprotected back.

Just before he can strike, Sergius acts. The gladiator has spent the last quarter hour lulling his opponent into a false sense of superiority and has been getting mightily annoyed during the process. Even as the Thracian prepares to stab, Sergius punches upward with his shield. The boss of the shield is a bronze head of Medusa and, even though the Thracian is protected by the grille of his helmet, when an over-muscled 200lb gladiator punches with all his might, what he punches stays properly punched. Stunned, the Thracian falls to the ground, and to the cheers of the spectators Sergius places his foot on his opponent's throat in a symbolic gesture of victory.

'You didn't have to do that,' grumbles the Thracian afterwards. He sits on a stool in their impromptu changing room and waves a finger back and forth in front of his nose as he tests for concussion.

'Then you shouldn't have kept hitting my helmet,' snarls Sergius in reply. A slave girl is using a strigil to scrape the sweat from his body, and Sergius is being paid for this too. Gladiator sweat from a bout is a prized element in ladies' body oils and cosmetics, just as blood from a slain gladiator is sometimes put on the spearhead with which a Roman groom ceremonially parts his bride's hair. It is all a part of the gladiator mystique.

The Strigil

The Romans did not believe that sitting in a bathtub and getting sudsy was the proper route to cleanliness. Indeed, one did sit in a large bath, preferably in the company of friends, but the point of the exercise was to get the pores of the skin properly opened.

At this point you exited the bath and were suitably anointed with fragrant oil. Then, after you had marinated for a few minutes, the oil was scraped off the skin, taking with it any dirt, dead skin or other impediments to hygiene.

The scraper was called a *strigil*, a blunt, curved copper blade that could be operated by the occupant of the body but was ideally wielded by a servant or a comely slave. Later eras have many examples of well-preserved strigils, because the connotations with cleansing and purification meant that they were often symbolically buried with the deceased.

Later, Sergius will ponder this as, wearing a clean tunic, he heads even further up the Caelian Hill for his final job of the evening. A far from unpleasant task awaits. The lady Eppia has tired of sleeping alone while her aristocratic husband travels abroad with the court of his peripatetic emperor Hadrian. Aware that his wife might stray, the husband has placed watchmen at her door. However, as the poet Juvenal has remarked: 'All the time my old friends advise, "Secure the doors and keep your wife behind them." Yes indeed, but who will guard the guards?'

For a generous remuneration, Sergius will be spending the night with this lady. What, he wonders, does she see in him that she allows herself to be called 'gladiator meat'? His face is misshapen and battered, and his helmet has left a permanent scar on his forehead. There's a steady trickle from one eye after an old injury, and a weeping ulcer on his arm.

But then, as Juvenal also points out, 'He is a gladiator! It is this she prefers to children and family. What these women love is the sword!'[15]

Hermes is the toast of the town in martial contests,
Hermes is skilled with every weapon,
Hermes is a gladiator; the master gladiator.

Hermes terrorizes and awes his entire school!
...
Hermes is the object of care and anxiety to the actresses.
Hermes of the proud and warlike spear.

Hermes threatens with Neptune's trident.
Hermes the terrible, with his face-hiding helmet.
Hermes, in every way the glory of Mars
Everything in himself and three times a man.

MARTIAL *Epigrams* 5.24

▥ HORA NOCTIS V ▥
(23.00–00.00)

THE PARASITE RETURNS
FROM DINNER

Yes, I'm fishing for an invitation for dinner with you,
I am embarrassed about it,
And yet, Maximus, I'm still fishing.

MARTIAL *Epigrams* 2.18

It is late, and the moon is setting below the rooftops as the parasite makes his way homeward, dinner clothes bundled under one arm and a bulging napkin of snacks, rolls and sundry delicacies clutched like a bag of booty in the other. 'Selius the Sponge', they call him, and – mellowed by his host's good food and wine – Selius wonders if that's really such an insult.

Okay, he's a parasite – that is, a '*para sitos*', which is from Greek and means 'fellow diner'. It's also true that the others at the dinner rather look down on him because, rather like the flute girls during the meal and the gladiators afterwards, he's less one of the guests at the table and more part of the accompanying entertainment. No one invites a boring parasite to dinner; Selius has to earn his meal by being witty, delivering elegant jokes and quoting obscure poetry. He must outshine the others around the table with his style and ingenuity, and yet this must all seem uncontrived and spontaneous.

Is this not then an art? A profession? Consider, Selius muses as he tramps along, what is the fate of an untrained sailor? He drowns. A soldier unskilled at arms is quickly slain. An artist, a sculptor, who lacks skill and training finds no clients. He perishes for want of employment. It is just so with a parasite – if he cannot talk his way into a dinner, he starves.

In fact, the sponger is more accomplished an artist than, say, a painter or a poet. A poet may go days or weeks without producing a decent epigram, and a painter might let his art languish between commissions. Yet if Selius is not on the top of his game, and refining his skills by practising his art nightly, then without this daily exercise of his ability his art would perish, and he with it. That said, Selius has to admit – with an internal wince – tonight was not his finest hour.

Curse that Manidus, and his evil sense of humour! Selius calls Manidus a 'friend' because he has previously been a fellow guest at dinners with the man, and has also previously attended one of his dinner parties. And as the writer Lucian has declaimed:[16]

Well, you wouldn't invite an enemy, a stranger or even a casual acquaintance to dinner. He has to be a friend before whom you can break bread and dine, and confide in him your secrets.

Have you never heard people say, 'Friend? How can he call
himself a friend if he has never dined or drunk with us.' I know
I have heard this.

A man's only to be trusted if you have dined with him.

LUCIAN *Parasitos* 22

The previous afternoon, while at the Baths of Trajan, Selius had happened upon Manidus in conversation with a companion. The word 'Cyrene' came up, and Selius leapt at the opening.

'Cyrene? A magnificent and exotic place! Have you been there? There is so much to know, so much to tell, about that great city. Ah, Africa – *ex Africa aliquid semper novi*. Anything new always comes from there. You would be amazed by what there is to know about Cyrene.'

Amused by this rhapsodizing, Manidus promptly invited Selius to dinner the following day, so that, 'You can tell us all about it.' The delighted Selius had immediately accepted the invitation, and then taken his leave as soon as decently possible to rush from the Baths of Trajan to the Library of Trajan at the foot of the Esquiline Hill, there to study as much about Cyrene as he possibly could. For, in reality, Selius has barely set foot outside of Rome. Country air gives him hay fever.

$\longleftarrow \qquad\qquad\qquad\qquad\qquad\qquad \longrightarrow$

If he sees the threat of having to dine at home
Selius leaves no stone unturned.
He'll hurry from one landmark to the next,
Not just to the civic buildings and temples of Rome,
but even to insalubrious bathhouses.

In his desperation he bathes three times in the public baths.

*Still unsuccessful, he rushes back to where he started at the
Portico of Europa.*

Perhaps there he will bump into an acquaintance who is out late.

*For heaven's sake, Bull of Jupiter, won't you carry Selius off
to dinner?*

Martial *Epigrams* 2.14

The dinner started well. Who could match him in joking or in his keen appreciation of the chef's abilities? Who else could so have relaxed his fellow diners with an apposite observation, a shrewd compliment or deprecating humour? It's what he does. As they say, with those who practise most professions, their times of enjoyment are two or three times a month; for the professional parasite, every evening is a feast.

The problem came along with the sweetcakes, when Manidus had folded his napkin and innocently asked about Cyrene. Selius immediately launched into his homework.

'For the perilous voyage,' he began his declamation, 'I took ship from Ostia.'

Immediately, the bearded Syrian gent at the top couch looked interested. 'Really?' he asked. 'What ship? Most of the trade to Cyrene goes through Puetoli. If there's someone who sails from Ostia I'd like to know him.'

Things went downhill from there. It quickly became apparent that the Syrian was a spice trader who knew Cyrene and the eastern Mediterranean as well as Selius knows the way to his own latrine. Selius writhes mentally at the memory of Manidus dabbing his lips with a napkin to hide his smile as the trader gently corrected him at every turn. 'Flocks of ibex flying into the sunset? Do you perhaps mean ibis? It's just that ibex are a kind of antelope and not very aerodynamic.'

SLAVES ATTEND TO A DINER IN THIS MOSAIC

'Your meal was flavoured with silphium? How wonderful that they have rediscovered a supply of the plant! Everyone thought it had been extinct these last hundred years. And you ate it at the taverna of Tingitus by the harbour? That is excellent news. I was told it had burned down a few years ago. I am delighted to hear it has been rebuilt.'

By now it was clear to Selius that the spice trader was on to him as a fraud, yet Manidus kept sadistically pressing for details. 'So you told us yesterday that you have actually met one of the famous Sciapodes? Do these strange one-legged people really lie on their backs in the midday sun and use their one huge foot as a sunshade? ... Oh dear, it appears that my friend here has come down with a coughing fit. Do let me attend to him before you tell us about it.'

There is a tribe of men [in Ethiopia] called the One-Legged, who have indeed only one leg. They jump along and move at a remarkable speed. This race of people are also called Sciapodes – the shadow feet – because in the hotter weather they lie on their backs on the ground and shade themselves with their feet.

PLINY THE ELDER *Natural History* 7.23

Torture. That's what it was, pure and simple torture. Indeed, as he was leaving, one of the other guests had sympathetically remarked that it had been a lot less painful to watch the gladiators getting whacked about the head in the after-dinner exhibition bout. Well, Selius is not going to stand for it. Next time Manidus asks him to dinner, he just won't go.

Can't he see that a rich man, even if he has all the gold of Croesus, is still poor if he dines alone? Who then will compliment him on the richness of his furnishings, the splendour of his *triclinium*, the handsomeness of his attendants? A soldier without his weapons, a horse without its trappings – that's a rich man at table without a parasite as a guest. He makes a poor, mean spectacle. No, the patron needs the parasite more than the parasite needs the patron. Sooner serve a meal without salt than have company unleavened by a parasite's charm and wit.

The sponger – when not being cross-examined about Cyrenean trivia – is a cheerful, carefree soul. He has no cook to be angry with, no country farm with foremen and harvests to let him down. He is the one man at the table who can eat and drink without the worries that the others cannot escape. Consider the strained relations so evident between cook and hostess at tonight's meal. If you are the host and the cook disappoints you, you must either put up with his sulking or else purchase peace and quiet by eating badly and missing your pleasure. Not Selius, who samples the work of a different cook every night. Therefore, thinks Selius, I offer you, Manidus, the *digitus impudicus*, that obscene gesture with the middle finger indicative of contempt and disdain. I don't need this.

As Selius was leaving the Manidus household, the wife had muttered to her husband – making no attempt to prevent him from hearing – 'That was a disaster. Next time, invite a philosopher.'

You go unwillingly to this dinner –
Or so you say, Classicus
And I'll be hanged if you aren't lying!

Apicius [Rome's master chef] was glad enough to go eating out
and he was miserable when he dined at home.
So if you go unwillingly, Classicus,
Why do you go at all?

'I'm obliged to go,' you say.
Sure you are, just as Selius is obliged.

Now Melior has invited you to a splendid banquet,
And where are your fine protestations?
Put your stomach where your mouth is,
And refuse to go.

MARTIAL *Epigrams* 2.69

Sure, thinks Selius, that will work. Who would you want at dinner – someone who works hard to be the life and soul of the party, or a man without a single chuckle in his bones, who sits there in a threadbare cloak with his eyes on the ground as though he were at a funeral and not a dinner party. Maybe Her Dragoness is thinking of inviting an Epicurean – after all, the followers of Epicurus are meant to consider happiness the greatest good, and fine foods and wine can go a long way towards encouraging this feeling.

Personally, Selius feels that where happiness is concerned the Epicureans have taken a leaf from the parasite's own handbook. Deep in his meditations, and with his thoughts slightly fuddled by wine, Selius automatically takes a right as he comes to the Velia and starts heading slightly uphill towards his rooms on the lower Viminal Hill.

He mutters to himself, 'It's pure larceny, the philosophers aspiring to happiness. I mean, what is happiness, when you come down to it? I take it that happiness is an untroubled soul in a body at peace with itself. So who has that? Is it the man who is constantly enquiring into the shape of the earth, whether space is infinite and the size of the sun? Do I grapple with astronomical distances, the nature of the elements, the existence or non-existence of the gods, or do I engage in incessant controversies with my colleagues? That's your philosopher. I, once I've arranged my next dinner, am convinced that I'm living in the best of all possible worlds. Once my stomach is satisfied, my hands and feet can look after themselves. Philosophers, hah! They have no place in a decent dining room.'

So preoccupied is Selius with his internal diatribe that he walks straight into a group of youths going the other way. There's a violent collision, and the inevitable recriminations. Looking at the angry faces, Selius realizes he has a problem. These young men have been to a party, and he recognizes the sort of fellows who can only sleep after they've had a brawl. If you can call it a brawl, when he'll take all the blows and they'll do all the thrashing.

'Who ate the beans that blew you out of his backside?' demands one of these louts, advancing threateningly. He sees the dinner garments clamped under Selius' arm and hoots with laughter. 'With what cobbler have you been chomping through cut leeks and boiled sheep's head, hey? Answer me, or take – that – in your shins!'

Selius leaps back in alarm. By now he's praying that he will make it home with a few teeth left in his head. 'Now, boys … ,' he says ingratiatingly, and looks again at the large and shadowy forms advancing towards him. Where are the vigiles when you need them?

Coming to an instant decision, Selius flings his napkin full of treats at the party and flees down the street, his sandals flapping loudly on the flagstones. He vanishes into the shadows followed by mocking laughter and shouts of abuse, but to his huge relief no one makes any serious effort to follow him.

The youths, talking loudly, make their way on down towards the Forum, and eventually peace returns. In the stillness, a stray cat emerges from the shadows to investigate the dropped foodstuffs on the road and quietly begins to eat. Above the now-silent street, the stars glow in the midnight black of the sky. And while the city slumbers, the slow wheeling of the constellations carries Rome into another day.

ENDNOTES

THE SLAVE GIRL PREPARES BREAKFAST

1 This method of telling the time by the stars can still be used today, as the constellations have changed only in their names. The Dog's Tail is now Polaris, the Pole Star, while the Seven Oxen have become the Plough to Europeans, and the Big Dipper to Americans.

THE MOTHER CARES FOR HER SICK BABY

2 Antiphon 87 B. 49d

3 Cicero, *Tusculan Disputations* 5.2.413

4 *Epistulae* 99.2

THE SCHOOLBOY STARTS MORNING CLASS

5 *Satire* 7.203ff

THE TEENAGER BREAKS UP WITH HER BOYFRIEND

6 Sulpicia 2,7–8

THE STONEMASON WORKS ON AN IMPERIAL TOMB

7 In fact, this is a false etymology, but a contemporary error rather than a modern one

THE TAVERN KEEPER

8 The incident at the Ninth Pillar tavern described by Copa at the start of the hour is that related (with more obscenities) by the poet Catullus in *Carmina* 37. Copa's story follows his account so closely that some of Catullus' lines are repeated almost verbatim.

9 Other graffiti from Pompeii, such as the dice players and the warning to patrons to keep their hands off the serving girls, have been made a part of Copa's story.

The Bath Attendant Checks in Customers

10 Martial *Epigrams* 7.88

11 Juvenal *Satire* 2

The Washerwomen Does a Late Shift

12 The owl symbolizes Minerva, the patron god of fullers. 'Arms and the Man' is the opening line of Vergil's famous *Aeneid*.

13 Because of this, public urinals in Paris were until recently called *Vespasiennes*.

The Spice Trader Sets Out for Dinner

14 In fact, at noon in Cape Town, South Africa, as you look west, the noon sun is indeed on your right – i.e. to the north, just as in the northern hemisphere the noon sun is to the left.

The Gladiator Struts His Stuff

15 Both Juvenal *Satire* 6.347

The Parasite Returns from Dinner

16 Apologies to Lucian of Samosata (AD 125–180), whose lawyers are doubtless sharpening their pens to file a copyright writ against Selius, since most of his philosophizing and rambling is lifted directly from Lucian's satirical dialogue *The Parasite*. Likewise, the encounter and dialogue with the street thugs comes almost verbatim from Juvenal's third *Satire*.

Picture Acknowledgements

Model of a Roman fire engine (page 14), Mary Evans Picture Library

Mosaic of two-wheeled cart (page 27), MuseoPics – Paul Williams / Alamy

Pomepeian bakery (page 32), photo Jeremy Day

Mistress and slave girl (page 48), Werner Forman / Universal Images Group / Getty Images

Post natal scene from Roman bas relief (page 55), Mary Evans Picture Library

The slow mail (page 63), Johann Jaritz / Creative Commons CC-by-SA-3.0

Roman students in formal dress (page 73), photo Philip Matyszak, from the Vatican Museum

Roman senators on parade (page 83), DEA / G Dagli Orti / Getty Images

Vestal Virgin (page 95) Art Media / Print Collector / Getty Images

The Basilica at Pompei (page 105), martin951 / Shutterstock.com

Girl playing knucklebones (page 117), Carole Raddato / Creative Commons CC-by-SA-2.0

Stonemason with his tools (page 127), Azoor Photo / Alamy

Statuette of a Dancer (page 139), J. Paul Getty Museum / Gift of Barbara and Lawrence Fleischman

Water clock (page 144), Nicku / Shutterstock.com

Bath house interior (page 154), Photo Jeremy Day

Roman sideboard (page 164), illustration from *The Private Life of the Romans* by Harold W. Johnston; Scott, Foresman and Co., Chicago 1903

Roman lady (page 166), DEA / De Agostini / Getty Images

Roman laundry (page 178), photo Jeremy Day

Buying hares at market stall (page 184), Museo Ostiense, Ostia Antica, Rome

Priestess statue (page 196), photo Jeremy Day

Spices on the move (page 207), DEA / G. Dagli Orti / Getty Images

Prostitute (page 217), Pecold / Shutterstock.com

Erotic Roman oil lamp (page 219), Anagoria / Creative Commons CC-by-3.0

Capricorn (page 228), woodcut from *Quaestio Virgiliana* by Francisci Campani, 1540

Mosaic showing gladiators (page 237), Leemage / Corbis via Getty Images

Gladiator statue (page 241), Granger / REX / Shutterstock

Slaves mosaic (page 249), The Bardo National Museum, Tunis

INDEX

A

Acetobacillus 39
Achilles 159
Aelia Sentia, law 109
Aelius, astrologer 229
Aemilius Paullus 199
Africa 75, 76, 195, 211, 233, 247
Agamemnon 146, 189
Agrippa 60, 62, 161, 233
  baths of 161
Alban hills 127
Alexander the Great 68, 208
Alexandria 15, 28, 30, 68, 150,
  203, 209, 230
Almagest, the 230
Alps, the 64
Alypius 240
Andromache 45
Antoninus, emperor (Antun)
  209, 234
Antony, Mark 199
Apennines, the 209
Apollo, god 79
Apollodorus of Damascus 160
Appian Way 21, 92
Appius Claudius 43
Aquae Sulis (Bath) 153
Aquincum 153
Arabia 165

Archimedes 145
Aristarchus of Samos 145
Ascletario, astrologer 231
Asia Minor 125, 149, 233, 240
Asia, western 208
Athens 150, 166
Attice 221
Atticus 167
Augustus, emperor 16, 62, 67, 105,
  111, 116, 123, 127-130, 161,
  164, 199, 232, 233
Aurelia, Via 60, 63

B

Ba'al, god 75, 195
Baiae 234
Balbilus, astromomers 224-229,
  231, 234
Barace 204
Bithynia 64
Blues chariot team 239
Borneo 207
Britain/Britannia 59, 62, 67, 68, 69,
  86, 136, 153, 207, 210, 233
Byzantium 28

C

Caesar (rank) 81, 128, 136, 236
Caesar, Julius 53, 123, 130, 225, 233

Caligula, emperor 199, 216
Calpurnia, wife of Pliny 114
Catullus, poet 240
Capitolina, Claudia astrologer 228
Cappadocia 30
Carthage 28
Castor, god (see also Pollux) 137
Cato the Elder 108
Cato the Stoic 164
Cattigara 207
Ceionius, Lucius Commodus 81,
    85-89, 93, 224, 225
Celer, slave (see Verus) 39
Centumcellae 66
Cerberus,watchdog 56
Cerealia festival 238
Cerealis, Velius 53
Ceylon (see Sri Lanka) 207
China 207, 208
Christians 61, 195, 198
Chthonic Gods 20
    Cicero, Marcus 56,
    Cicero, Quintus 167
Cilicia 68
Cimolian/cimolus earth
    177-179
Cinna 168
Classicus 251
Claudius, emperor 82, 228, 236
Cleopatra 199
Commodus (see Ceionius)
Cornelia 53

Cottonara 205
Crassus, Marcus Licinius 16
Croesus 250
Ctesibius of Alexandria 143
Cyrene 206, 207, 210, 247, 248

D

Dacia 7
    Dacian War 128
Danube, river 153
Daquin (Rome) 209
Dasius, bath attendant 160
Dictys 202
Domitian, emperor 199, 200,
    229, 231, 232

E

Egeria, nymph 92, 98, 99
Egypt 15, 30, 68, 131, 194, 199,
    200, 205, 209, 210, 230, 233
Ephesus 228
Epicurus/Epicureans 252
Epiphi (July) 205
Eppia 243
Erotion 56
Erythraean (Red) Sea 210
Ethiopia 250
Etruria 66
Euclid 230
Europe 23

F

Fisica, Venus 222
Flacilla 56
Flaminius 66
Flora, goddess 143, 219
Floralia, festival 200, 219
Florus 136,137
Fornax, goddess 190
Fronto 56
Fucine Lake 236
Fufidus 163

G

Gades (Cadiz) 240
Ganges, river 205
Gaul 68, 149, 207
Germany 62
Gibraltar 210
Granius Verus 39

H

Hadrian, emperor 7, 61, 63, 67,
    68, 79, 85, 86, 107, 123-125,
    128, 129, 136, 137, 155, 161,
    200, 225-229, 233, 234, 243
Hannibal 75
Hecate, goddess 20
Hector 45
Hecuba 77
Helica pomatia, snail 185
Helvidiae, sisters 53

Herculaneum 39,134
Hercules 210,214
Hermes, gladiator 244
Hermogenes 171
Herodotus of Halicarnassus
    125, 211
Hippalus, trade wind 209
Horace 71, 72, 164
Horus, god 197
Hostilius Mancinus 17

I

Ilithyia, goddess 50
India 62, 203-206, 208-210,
    217
Iris, slave 141
Isidore, saint 200
Isis (also Iset) 192-202, 208
Italica 227
Italy 63, 209

J

Janus, god 201
Java 210
Jerome, saint 112
Jews 192, 195, 197, 200
Juno, goddess 54
Jupiter 189, 195, 234, 248
Justinian, code of 112

K

Kerala 205

L

Larentia, Acca 213, 214, 218
Larentina, festival of 214
Latium 21
Legio V Macedonica 83
Legio XX Valeria Victrix 67
Leptis Magna 75
Lesbia 119
Levant, the 68
Licinius, Lucullus 164
Londinium (London) 66, 69
Lucina Genitalis, goddess 50
Lucius, *Golden Ass* 217
Lybia 211
Lycia 240

M

Macedonia 68
Mancinus, aedile 17, 219, 223
Manilius, astronomer 231, 232
Marathon, battle of 68
Mari 121
Marius, Caius 84
Mars, god 97, 201, 244
Marsyas 79
Massa 171
Mauricus, Junius 117
Mausolus of Halicarnassus 125

Maximus 245
Mediolanum (Milan) 64, 74
Medusa 242
Megasthenes, geographer 208
Melior 251
Menogenes 159
Mercury, god 20, 69
Mesopotamia 7
Mesouranema, the 229
Minicius, Acilianus 117
Mira 204
Miyrandus 120
Mucius Scaevola 104
Municipalis, Lex 20, 28
Muza 208
Muziris, India 209
Myrtalis 132, 133

N

Neacindi 209
Neptune, god 161 (basilica – see Rome)
Nero, emperor 13, 137, 155, 160, 199, 211, 228
   Baths of 154, 161
Nerva, emperor 128
New York 101
Niger, river 210
Nile, river 209, 210
Numa Pompilius, king 93, 96, 99, 100

O

Ocelis, port 208, 209
Olympians, the 176
Onesicritus 208
Opimius 140
Osiris, god 196, 202
Ostia, port 28, 68, 204, 248

P

Paleogoni 208
Pannonia 153
Papian Law 93
Parian marble 127
Pericles 166
Persia 68
Persicus 22
Peutinger, map 62
Philae 194
Picenum 22, 37
Plautus 142
Plotius, Lucius Voltacilius 76
Pluto, god 20
Po, river 209
Pollux (see also Castor) 137
Pompeii 172, 210
Pompey the Great 123
Pomponia 167
Prima, bar of 141
Psecas 45
Ptolemaic Universe 230, 232
Ptolemy, Claudius astrologer
  230-233

Puetoli 248

R

Remus 97
Rhine, river 138
Rinan see vietnam 209
Rome (Daquin)
  Aelian Bridge 129
  Aemilian bridge 115
  agger, the 96
  Aqua Appia 19, 24
  Aqua Virgo 161
  Aventine Hill 17, 19, 21, 25, 26,
  28-30, 33, 38, 162
  Basilica of Neptune 161
  Caelian Hill 180, 211, 220, 240,
  243
  Campus Martius 122, 123, 128,
  154, 161, 197
  Capentian Gate 92, 99
  Capitoline hill 59, 92, 100
  Cariniae, the 220
  Circus Maximus 12, 13, 19, 124
  Colline Gate 96
  Colosseum 97, 127, 151, 184,
  220, 237, 241
  Esquiline Hill 26, 134, 220, 220,
  247
  Flavian Amphitheatre 127 (see
  also Colosseum)
  Holitorium, forum 26, 113
  Horologium, the 130, 131

Iseum Campense 197

Mausoleum of Hadrian 125, 128, of Augustus 128-131

Mercatus, Via 21

Oppian Hill 160

Ostia Gate 19

Palatine hill 26, 61, 68, 100, 131

Pantheon 123, 154, 161

Patricus, Via 17

Portico of Europa 248

Portico of Octavia (the Basilica) 70, 71, 74, 76, 80, 104, 114, 115

Tullianum, the 109

Regio II 12

Subarra 220

Tabularium records office 59, 63

Tarpeian Rock 92

Tiber 28, 60, 94, 109, 123, 129, 173, 187, 197, 199, 201

Transtiberim district 60, 173

Velia, the 252

Viminal hill 26, 252

Romulus 97, 213

S

Sahara desert 232

Salinator, Pedanius Fuscus 225

Salonia (see also Cato) 165

Sarda earth 178

Sardinia 178

Saturnalia festival 21, 97, 138, 143, 238

Sciapodes 249, 250

Scipio Africanus 53

Seneca 57, 228

Serapis, god 197

Servi (see Sulpicia) 121

Seville 200

Sextilanus 140

Sicily 149

Sinus Magnus 207

Sirius (Dog Star) 208

Spain 28, 81, 185, 227

Spatale 160

Sri Lanka 62, 207
   Celon, Serendib,
      Taprobane 62, 207, 208

Statius 167

Successus 141

Syria 203, 208, 210

T

Tacitus 13, 216

Tarquinium 66

Tetrabiblos, the 230

Thames, river 7

Theogenes, astrologer 233

Theon of Smyrna 230

Thrasyllus, astrologer 228, 231

Thule 210

Tiberius, emperor 105, 137, 199, 228

Tibur 22

Tigris, river 7

Titus Flavius, Emperor
175, 200
Toma 86, 87
Trajan, emperor 30, 64, 65, 124,
128, 161,
Baths of 160, 247
Library of 247
Trebius 90
Trimalchio 146, 156, 188, 189
Tuccia 94, 96

U

Ululitremulus, Fabius 172
Uranus, planet 227
Urban Cohorts 17
Ursa minor 42

V

Venus Goddess 118, 126, 217, 226
Verginia 43
Verus, Quintus Granius (see also
Celer) 39
Vespasian, emperor 128, 129, 151,
175, 199, 200, 228, 229
Vesta, Goddess 92-94, 96, 97, 99,
100
Vestals 92-94, 96-100, 241
Vesuvius, Mt 39
Vettius Pompustius 229
Vienna 62
Vietnam also Rinan 209
Vigiles 12, 14-19, 25, 26, 253

Vindictus 108
Visitilia 216
Vulcan 152

W

Wines
Pelignian, Tuscan, Laletan 140,
Greek 168, Mamertine 168,
Massic 140, 168

Roman Magistrates and Officials

Consul 81, 82, 92, 199, 228

Praetor 104, 106–111, 114, 115, 119, 122

Aedile curule and plebeian 17, 18, 81, 84, 215, 219

Tribune 92, 94, 223

Pontifex Maximus 97

Curiae 100

Characters Invented or Partly Fictionalized by the Author

Aelia, society lady 163

Albinus, Marcus 114, 119, 120, 121

Albinus, Clockmaker 145-147, 149, 150

Brevis, Petronius, watchman 11-13, 15-18

Caecilius Septimius, cook 172, 173, 180-188, 190-193

Casce 75, 76

Cerinthus 114-118, 119, 120, 121

Copa, inkeeper 132-138, 140, 142, 145-147, 150, 151

Curius, Lucius 50, 52, 54-56, 58

Gaius the Jurist 104-111

Gallienus Postumus, stonemason 124-128, 130-132

Hypsates, Julius 84

Licinia, hostess 54, 164-168, 170, 171, 182, 184, 186, 188, 190, 204, 206

Macrius, Titus Aulus the messenger 59-69

Manidus, Marcus Aulus 162-168, 170, 172, 182, 183, 188, 203, 204, 206, 212, 246-249, 250, 251

Mamila, prostitute 18, 213-216, 218, 219, 220-223

Marcia, Vestal Virgin 91, 92, 94, 97-102, 104

Misthrathius, baker 29-31, 33-38

Miyria, teenager 113-116, 118-122

Miyrius, spice trader 120, 121, 203-212

Ofella, Mamlius Aurelius, senator 80-94, 224-227, 230, 231, 234

Orbilius 71, 74-76, 78, 79

Publius Phelyssam, schoolboy 70-72, 75-79

Sergius the Gladiator 235-244

Thais, washerwoman 172-177, 179-181, 191

Tingitus, Taverna of 249

Seius, the parasite 236-245

Seluca 163, 170

Syricus 216, 218

Sosipatra, the mother 50-58 (see also Termalis, Termalia

Syrisca, bar-girl 133-136, 140

Vibius, Caius the Carter 20-26, 28

SOURCES

Antigonus of Nicea:
  Astronomica 229
Augustine: *Confessions* 241
Aurelius Marcus: *Meditations* 224
Aelius Spartianus/*Historia Augusta:
  Life of Hadrian
  Historia Augusta* 137, 234
Anon
  Philogelos 220, *Periplus of the Red
  Sea* 205
Apicius: *Recipes* 186, 205, 251
Apuleius: *The Golden Ass* 33, 177,
  194, 198, 218
Ausonius: *Moselle* 152
Cassius Dio: *History* 129, 130
Cato: *De Agricultura* 28, 187
Catullus: *Carmina* 113, 119
Cicero: *Letters to Atticus* 167,
  Pro Caelio 213
Corpus Inscriptiones Latinarum
  58, 134, 141, 172, 173,
  221, 222
Dionysius of Halicarnassus: *Roman
  Antiquities* 100
Epictetus: *Discourses* 82
Gaius: *Institutes* 112
Gellius Aulus: *Noctes Atticae* 93,
  142, 223
Horace: *Epodes* 50
Hou Hanshu: *Chronicle* 209
Juvenal: *Satires* 19, 20, 22, 30, 45,
72, 75, 78, 90, 150, 156, 157,
183, 243, 244
Lactantius: *Institutiones Divinae*
  219
Livy: *Ab Urbe Condida* 43, 227
Lucian: *Parasitos* 246 (cf much of
  Hora Noctis V)
Lucretius: *On the Nature of Things*
  80
Martial: *Epigrams* 37, 70, 79, 140,
  159, 160, 168, 171, 179, 182,
  244, 245, 248, 251
Ovid: *Ars Amatoria* 116
Petronius: *Satyricon* 146, 156, 189
Pliny the Elder 9
  Natural History 34-36, 54, 173,
  179, 203, 206, 208, 210, 250
Pliny the Younger: *Letters* 53, 64,
  65, 75, 114, 117, 169
Plutarch
  Lives: *Caesar* 226, Crassus 16,
    Marius 84, Numa 96; On Isis and
    Osiris 196, 202, Moralia 202,
Propertius and Tibullus: *Elegies*
  116, 132 (see Sulpicia)
Pseudo-Vergil: *Copa* 135
Quintillian: *Education of an Orator*
  78
Seneca (the younger)
  De Beneficiis 87, Letters 158
Soranus: *On Gynaecology* 52
Strabo: *Geography* 123, 210

Suetonius
  On Rhetoricians 76, Lives;
  Augustus 49, 233, *Caligula* 216,
  Claudius 236, *Vespasian* 175
Sulpicia (see Tibullus Propertius)
  116, 118, 120, 121
Tibullus see Sulpicia
Virgil: *Aeneid* 72, 76
Vitruvius: *De Architectura*
  147, 149

LATIN TERMS
IN THE TEXT

amicus 88, 89
ancilla ornatrice 215
auctoratus 236
balena 153
baletus 241
ballistae 15
balneum 152
bulla 78
caldarium 155, 156
calamistrum 44
clepsydra 143
cliens 88, 89
coniuratio 111
copa 135
cursus publicus 62, 64, 65
curule chair 106
defrutum 186
delicata 214
digitus impudicus 251

dorides 221
emporium 28, 210
farina 35
fasces 82, 88
feli arbor 97
fornes 220
frigidarium 155
fructarii 22
fullonica 172, 173, 175, 191
galina 216
garum 164, 185, 186
gentilictum 164
hoplomachus 238
Ides 225, 226, 234
kalends 225
lanista 235
legate 67
leno 18
libellus 105, 120
licentia stupri 216
lictors 88, 106
liquamen 185
litteratus 70, 71, 75, 78
Lupara 22, 135, 213, 218
macella 21
Mare clausum 28
mola 94
mormylos 238
mansio 62, 66, 68
materfamilias 53, 166, 167,
  170, 173
murmillo 237, 238

mutationes 64, 65, 66

nonaria 219

nundinum 21, 23, 26, 28

onagers 15

palestra 157

panissordidus 30

Parasitos 245, 247

paterfamilias 42, 78, 162

pedagogus 71-74

peponarii 22

pharmaka 42

pilaster 149

pilentum 91

Piscarium 11

plagosus 71

plaustrum 23, 25

pollice verso 238

pomerium 199

popina 135

quadriga 125

siligineus 35

silphium 249

rudis 237

speculatores 68

Speusticus 36

stola 100, 113, 180

stratorus 60, 65, 66

*strigi*l 156, 242, 243

tabellarius 60

taberna 64,
  blandita 136

tepidarium 155

tetrapharmacum 183, 186, 187

thermae 153

tholos 130

toga candida 177, 178

triclinium 163, 168, 250

tunica molesta 103

verna 42, 43

villicus puellarum 215

viripotens 215

Bibliography

Key texts consulted by the author

Adkins, L & Adkins, R. *Handbook to Life in Ancient Rome* 1998

Dudley, D. *Urbs Roma* 1967

Crook, J. *Law and Life of Rome* 1967

Gaius, (E.Post trans.) *The Institutes of Roman Law* 2017

Joshel, S. *Work, Identity, and Legal Status at Rome: a Study of the Occupational Inscriptions* 1992

McGinn, T. *The economy of prostitution in the Roman world: a study of social history & the brothel* 2004

Nippel, W. 'Policing Rome', *Journal of Roman Studies* 74 (1984) 20-29

Platner, S. *A Topographical Dictionary of Ancient Rome* 2015

Potter, D. and Mattingly, D. (eds) *Life, Death, and Entertainment in the Roman Empire* 1999

Rainbird, J. 'The fire stations of imperial Rome', *Papers of the British School at Rome* 41 (1986) 147-169.

Rich. A. *Dictionary of Roman and Greek Antiquities* 1860

Rawson, B. (ed.) *Marriage, Divorce and Children in Ancient Rome* 1991

Treggiari, S. *Roman Social History* 2002

Veyne, P. (B. Pearce trans.) *Bread and Circuses: Historical Sociology and Political Pluralism* 1990

Recommended Further Reading

Casson, L. *Everyday Life in Ancient Rome* 1999

Coletta, G. *Rome: Reconstructed* 2007

Edwards, C. & Woolf, G., (eds) *Rome the Cosmopolis* 2003

Harvey, B. *Roman Lives, Corrected Edition: Ancient Roman Life Illustrated by Latin Inscriptions* 2015

Matyszak, P. *Ancient Rome on 5 Denarii a Day* 2006

Stambaugh, J. *The Ancient Roman City* 1988